# Good and Plenty

# Good & Plenty

## The Creative Successes
## of American Arts Funding

## Tyler Cowen

*Princeton University Press*
*Princeton and Oxford*

Published by Princeton University Press, 41 William Street, Princeton,
New Jersey 08540
In the United Kingdom: Princeton University Press,
3 Market Place, Woodstock, Oxfordshire OX20 1SY

Library of Congress Cataloging-in-Publication Data

Cowen, Tyler.
    Good and plenty : the creative successes of American arts funding / Tyler Cowen.
        p.   cm.
    Includes bibliographical references and index.
    ISBN-13: 978-0-691-12042-3
    ISBN-10: 0-691-12042-0 (hardcover : alk. paper)
  1. United States—Cultural policy.   2. Art and State—United states.
3. Federal aid to the arts—United States.   4. Aesthetics—Economic aspects.
5. Culture—Economic aspects.   I. Title.
    NX735.C68  2006
    700.79'73—dc22
    2005030005

British Library Cataloging-in-Publication Data is available

This book has been composed in Electra.

Printed on acid-free paper. ∞

pup.princeton.edu

Printed in the United States of America

1 3 5 7 9 10 8 6 4 2

# Contents

# Acknowledgments

Tom Bradshaw, Bryan Caplan, Dana Gioia, Robin Hanson, Eli Lehrer, and Titus Levi have offered very useful comments and discussions. I also thank Peter Dougherty, Tim Sullivan, and several anonymous referees for their comments. Comments from readers of my earlier books on culture have proven useful as well. I also have benefited from a large number of comments at various presentations of this material over the last several years. Eric Crampton and Clark Durant have provided very useful research assistance. The Mercatus Center provided very useful research support.

Good and Plenty

# 1. Warring Perspectives

Many of my conservative and libertarian friends find government funding for the arts unacceptable. They note that after the so-called "Gingrich revolution" of 1994, "we were not even able to get rid of the NEA." They speak of the NEA (National Endowment for the Arts) as the lowest of lows, the one government program that has no justification whatsoever. If such an obvious basket case could survive a conservative Republican Congress, how we can ever hope to rein in government spending?

Most of my arts friends take the contrary political position. They assume that any art lover will favor higher levels of direct government funding. To oversimplify a bit, their basic attitude is that the arts are good, and therefore government funding for the arts is good. They find it difficult to understand how an individual can appreciate the arts without favoring greater public-sector involvement. They lament how American artists are underfunded and undervalued by the state, relative to their western European counterparts.

Why are the two sides to this debate so far apart? How can two groups of people, each well intentioned, look at the same world and see such a different reality?

That people so frequently disagree is a quandary for social science. We might expect that when a person encounters a disagreement with someone, he or she recognizes that the other person, if sufficiently intelligent and honest, is as likely to be right. To paraphrase Garrison

Keillor, we cannot all be in the top half of our peer group with regard to wisdom, and presumably we realize this. Furthermore our disputants often have superior training, experience, or raw intelligence. The reality, however, is that convergence of opinion is rare on most political issues. Policy disagreements usually persist, and often deepen, when the individuals engage in sustained personal dialogue. Furthermore the presentation of evidence and the citation of expert opinion usually fail to resolve the dispute.

I write with one foot in the art-lover camp and with another foot in the libertarian economist camp. I try to make each position intelligible, and perhaps even sympathetic (if not convincing), to the other side. I try to show how the other side might believe what it does, and how close the two views might be brought together. Furthermore, I use the fact of persistent disagreement as a kind of datum, as a clue for discovering what the issues are really about.

Except for the 1990s squabbles over the NEA, serious political dialogue on arts policy has simply not taken place. Presidential and congressional candidates prefer not to devote their attention to the issue, except for previous attempts to attack a few controversial grants.

I try to steer the arts policy debate away from its previous focus on the NEA. More significant questions concern the use of our tax system to support nonprofits, creating a favorable climate for philanthropy, the legal treatment of the arts, the arts in the American university, and the evolution of copyright law. I also seek to recast the debate over direct funding of the arts. The central issue is not, as many people suppose, how much money a given governmental agency should receive. It is hard to generate consensus on a question of this kind. Instead a more fruitful inquiry involves what general steps a government can take to promote a wide variety of healthy and diverse funding sources for the arts. For instance should we look more toward direct subsidies or indirect subsidies?

Most of all, arts policy is a window onto how the United States supports creative endeavors. It is commonly believed that we have no arts policy, and on one obvious level this claim is true. No central cabinet-level ministry plans the development of the American arts. At the same time, American governments, at varying levels, have done much to support creative enterprise. The American model arguably mobilizes government more effectively than do many of the European models for arts support. We are further from artistic laissez-faire than is commonly believed to be the case.

I will argue a case for the American system, at least once it is properly understood. The American model encourages artistic creativity, keeps the politicization of art to a minimum, and brings economics and aesthetics into a symbiotic relationship. That being said, the model is not necessarily preferable for all other countries, especially those that trade with the United States and already reap benefits from the American system. Furthermore I do not think it possible to defend each and every aspect of American arts policy. My defense of the American system focuses on the most general features of that regime — capitalist wealth, competitive markets, decentralized and diverse sources of financial support, and indirect subsidies. In the final chapter I also will suggest some means for improving the American system. Insofar as we wish to use direct subsidies, we should restructure them to encourage greater innovation and a greater degree of decentralized support for the arts.[1]

Finally, arts policy brings into relief critical questions in both policy evaluation and political philosophy. Man is not just a thinking being; he is also an imagining being and a creating being. Cultural policy focuses our attention on how we resolve potential clashes between economic and aesthetic values. Here more than just the arts is on the table. Our ability to reconcile economic and aesthetic values is a general prerequisite of rational policy evaluation.

Moving to yet larger questions, we cannot have a coherent political philosophy without bridging the gap between economic and aesthetic perspectives. For instance critics charge that liberalism cannot satisfy the higher aspirations of the human race. They compare liberal government to an innkeeper who looks after his guests but otherwise has little to offer in the way of vision or a common loyalty. On the international scene, the United States is often seen as a military and economic behemoth, but as lacking in concern for cultural values or beauty. I wish to put this picture to rest, and to reclaim America's rightful role in offering a liberal vision for beauty and creative human achievement.

I will use arts policy to begin a new sketch of a liberal state. The public sector can encourage a proliferation of diverse cultural outputs and in that regard offer a rich menu of life-enhancing options. At the same time, we do not have to abandon the values of free speech and neutrality across (noncoercive) competing lifestyles. All this can be done in a manner consistent with prosperity and other economic objectives. A state—in particular the American state—can be involved with matters aesthetic without losing its liberal character. We also will see that, counterintuitively, a rich diversity of artistic achievement is compatible with the ideas of cultural centrality and the use of culture to bind a polity together.[2]

Since the potential clash between economic and aesthetic perspectives is our central motivating concern, let us now turn to it more directly. We will look at policy evaluation at the microlevel, and then throughout the course of the book build back toward larger visions.

## Aesthetics and Economics

Neither the aesthetic approach nor the economic approach can stand alone as a tool for evaluating policy. Rather than try to elevate one approach at the expense of the other, I will look for policy recommendations that might reasonably persuade a person who assigned some validity to each perspective—economist and aesthete—at the same time.

The economic approach seeks to give consumers what they want. Many people watch *The Sopranos*, but few come home and pick up James Joyce's *Ulysses* after a day of hard work or even after a day of easy work. A book does not have to improve on successive rereadings if it will be read only once. Consumers care mostly about fun and convenience. A survey indicated that 46 percent of Americans would be unwilling to give up television for the rest of their lives in return for a million dollars.[3]

More technically, I define the economic approach in terms of standard microeconomics and Paretian welfare economics. Economists measure value in terms of willingness to pay or willingness to be paid.

The aesthetic approach favors products that will "last the ages." It points our attention to study-intensive classics and canonical works. It is harder to point to a single canonical presentation of the aesthetic approach, but I define the aesthetic view as suggesting that quality culture has intrinsic value. Matthew Arnold wrote that "culture is, or ought to be, the study and pursuit of perfection; and that of perfection as pursued by culture, beauty and intelligence, or in other words, sweetness and light."[4]

Under the aesthetic approach the notion of a just and beautiful society is prior to the value of satisfying individual preferences. Often a vision of "cultural democracy" is paramount. Art has elevating and developmental powers, and in this view all democratic citizens have a right to such experiences. Government is seen as capable of carving out a realm for human education and freedom, removed from negative commercial pressures. Without irony Hans Haacke wrote: "If culture is to remain free, we taxpayers must be ready to finance it!"[5]

Under the economic approach, high art is simply another minority taste and holds no special normative status. The economic approach treats the critic as simply another consumer, albeit with different intellectual and material endowments. A particular critic may be a consumer with time on his hands, an academic job, and special training in the classical piano repertoire. For the economist, this point of view is no more privileged than that of the consumer who works two jobs, has three small children, and never finished high school. Willingness to pay, rather than social standing, education, or any other variable, determines how much a person's preference is to be weighted. Along these lines, one study found that the American public had more respect for bus drivers and baseball players than for art critics (or poets, ballet dancers, or professional actors, for that matter).[6]

Often critics include popular culture in their canons. But they still judge popular culture from the perspective of a critic, rather than from the perspective of a consumer. These critics are trying to invest popular culture with the same qualities they have found in high culture. The critical commentary on *Seinfeld*, for instance, does not pursue the form that fan discussions of the show would take, such as who is the funniest character, whether Jerry and Elaine should reestablish a romantic relationship, or whether Kramer will get a job. It is possible to publish an academic article on "the postmodern in Seinfeld," but not on whether Elaine should have split up with her last boyfriend, although the latter is of greater concern to most of the show's viewers.

By siding with the consumer point of view, economics serves as a radical attempt to demystify the perspective of the critic. That is one reason why critics do not like the economic approach.

## The Problem of Commensurability

The aesthetic approach has a hard time making aesthetic values easily commensurable. It is difficult to decide whether Shakespeare's *Hamlet* is better than his *King Lear*, and even harder to persuade others of our decision or define what such a ranking would mean. How many Gershwin songs sum up to a Shostakovich symphony? Is a Haydn string quartet better than a Hemingway short story? How does a Blake poem compare to a modern ballet performance? When evaluating a government policy or a cultural era, do we look at the peaks that result, the total amount of art, or some weighted average of the two?

The average quality of output provides an inadequate standard of evaluation. The majority of artistic projects are commercial and aesthetic failures, regardless of the source of funds, the political system, or the time period. We care more about the successes than about the fate of every cultural undertaking. Similarly, we cannot judge government funding, or laissez-faire for that matter, by looking at the median or typical project. Anecdotes of failure can easily mislead. We should not be surprised if a particular system produces much junk and offensive material.

The most common benchmark uses "peaks" to compare one culture to another. Government funding is praised, for instance, for having supported Bach, Velázquez, and Edmund Spenser. The same invocation of peaks has been used to compare "the moderns" to "the ancients." We might ask what modern composer compares to Beethoven or what modern poem measures up to Homer's *Odyssey*. Or we might ask, "Which age has produced the best symphony?"

Yet the peaks standard demonstrates a potential bias against the market and prejudges significant, and open, aesthetic questions. Why should the greatness of the best composer, or the best poet, be the relevant unit for judging a culture? What if one culture (modernity?) produces lesser creative titans but produces many more of them? How are we to weigh the quality of the peak versus quantity of the total?

It is also an open question what is the right unit for judging a peak. Instead of looking at the highest peaks, we could judge an era by how good its "one hundred best composers" are, or by the aesthetic worth of its "best five thousand hours of music." Or consider a peak of a different kind: "How many excellent musical genres does an age have?" By these standards, contemporary times fare better, vis-à-vis the era of Beethoven, than if we just compare the best composer from each period. We have many talented composers today, in many different musical fields, even though today's best composer is not the equal of Beethoven.

Why the focus on a single artistic work and its greatness? Mozart's *Don Giovanni* has musical beauty, terror, comedy, and a sense of the sublime, making it a favorite of opera connoisseurs. But what if consumers draw their comedy from one work, their terror from another, their beautiful music from yet another, and so on? Artistic peaks typically bundle qualities together. Yet arguably a world with unbundled qualities is superior, since it allows consumers to pick and choose how much of each quality they want, and from which source.

We cite "peaks" when making an aesthetic assessment because they are relatively easy to observe and talk about. Few individuals know much about eighteenth-century culture except for its peaks. But the peaks standard remains incomplete. The notion of a peak does not correspond to how much aesthetic value is produced in an era or to how much that value is enjoyed.

The economic approach, whatever its weaknesses, has one major virtue. It makes aesthetic values commensurable, at least in principle. Individuals' willingness to pay gives us a standard, however crude, for how many Gershwin songs are worth a Haydn string quartet. So if individuals, taken collectively, are willing to pay $100,000 for a new Haydn recording, and $200,000 for a new Gershwin recording, the economic standard judges the Gershwin disc to be worth more. The economic approach rejects the dominance of aesthetic peaks per se. It looks instead at how much total value is produced, again as measured in monetary terms. Money is not all that counts, but all things that count are measured in terms of money.

The economic method therefore offers a practicable response to the awkward questions of how to define peaks, or how to weight quality versus quantity. This relatively straightforward approach to commensurability, no matter how much it horrifies the art purist, means the economic approach will be invoked repeatedly to adjudicate disputes. Analogously, philosopher and economist Henry Sidgwick argued that utilitarianism, whatever its apparent failings, was the only philosophy that could sensibly weigh competing values at the margin. Economics, a modern form of utilitarianism, offers a similar property. Perhaps the economic approach will be battered with telling and persuasive critiques. Yet it will reemerge in some form to address commensurability, even if it does not reign as the sole standard for judging policy.

The economic approach also holds a core of common sense at its center. Art lovers sometimes write or talk as if economic costs do not matter. They tend to evaluate regimes in terms of the quality of the art that is produced, without considering the opportunity costs of that art. More and better art is equated with a better society. We are never told how many bags of potato chips, or how many antipoverty programs, we should sacrifice to receive another great artistic performance, or how we might hope to find out such an answer. The economic approach reflects the view of the common man that art is not everything, or even the most important thing.

On the negative side, the economic approach considers only a limited range of values, namely those embodied in individual preferences and expressed in terms of willingness to pay. This postulate is self-evident to many economists, but it fails to command wider assent. It wishes to erect "satisfying a preference" as an independent ethical value but is unwilling to consider any possible competing values, apart from preferences. It is hard to see why nonpreference values should not be admitted to a broader decision calculus.

Typically economists retreat to their intuition that satisfying preferences is somehow "real," and that pursuing nonpreference values is religious, mystical, or paternalistic. The rest of the world, however, has not found this distinction persuasive. They do not see why satisfying preferences should be a value of special and sole importance, especially when those same preferences may be ill informed, inconsistent, malicious, or spiteful. The decisions to count all preferences, to use money as the measuring rod, and to weight all market demands equally must themselves rely on external ethical judgments. For that reason, the economist has no a priori means of dismissing nonpreference values from the overall policy evaluation.

Economists often accuse other methods of policy evaluation of paternalism, but this is more of an ad hominem attack than an argument. It is paternalism to force an alternative on society that nobody wants, or to force an individual to do something against her will. It is less clear why it is paternalistic to use nonpreference-based values as "tiebreakers." What if social preferences do not themselves suggest a clear or nearly unanimous rank ordering? Why is it so unreasonable to look to other values to resolve deadlocked preferences?

Economists have long treated merit goods as a kind of "add-on" to standard cost-benefit analysis. That is, we stick with standard cost-benefit methods and simply add on a value for the relevant merit good. By definition, a merit good is of greater value—for intrinsic reasons—than is reflected in individual preferences. This procedure, however, requires a common understanding on the relevant value trade-offs. It also requires that noneconomic values be squeezed into the economic framework. Many art lovers wish to keep the idea of the merit good but jettison the underlying economics.[7]

Some economists prefer contractarian ideas, to derive unanimity at a broader level of social choice. Yet we must specify what information and values people will have "behind the veil," thereby also determing what they would choose. We first need some prior theory of what is right, or some prior theory of what kind of life a self-interested person would pursue. But if we have significant prior knowledge about these questions, we should start with it directly. Such foundations, if present, would move us away from the economic approach.

The economic approach also performs best when the distribution of wealth is given, preferences are fixed and well defined, and the policy change in question is a small one. Perhaps economics can tell us whether we should build an extra stadium in St. Louis, but it is less well suited for analyzing the entirety of arts policy. Often art consumers do not know what they want until it is before them, which vitiates the fixed-preference assumption. The arts and thus arts policy are shaping what preferences will be. More generally, the supply of art helps determine what "languages" individuals will have at their command for interpreting social reality. The economic method, taken alone, is poorly suited for evaluating such choices.[8]

Pure Paretian improvements, which make everybody better off, are hard to come by. So for most practical purposes, applied welfare economics boils down to wealth maximization. But then we must wonder why wealth is such a supreme value. Even Richard Posner gave up his wealth maximization standard, in response to scathing criticism from Ronald Dworkin. Dworkin made the simple point that wealth cannot plausibly be an end in itself. Wealth may be a useful proxy for other values, such as justice, fairness, happiness, and beauty, but if so (and these connections are not self-evident), we should target these other values directly. These targets may be hard to measure, but if they were impossible to measure, we could not claim that wealth was a useful proxy for them. We would again have no rationale for the wealth maximization standard.[9]

Arthur Schlesinger, Jr., remarked that only "a moment's reflection" is needed to realize that the economic approach to arts policy is "absurd." While this is a gross overstatement, the economic approach has not won many debates in the philosophic arena.[10]

## How Do the Differing Approaches View Subsidies?

The aesthetic approach opens the door for a case for government subsidies to art. Few critics believe that market-driven culture will maximize its potential aesthetic value, or admit of no aesthetic improvements. The perspective of the critic therefore finds an obvious, and potentially remediable, flaw in market outcomes. To the extent that the government can use good taste to target outcomes, direct subsidies could improve on laissez-faire.

The economic framework, by adopting the perspective of consumers, leads to greater skepticism about subsidies. Consumers spend most of their cultural time with commercially viable products. They watch television, buy popular novels, and listen to popular music; esoteric forms of high culture are of less interest to them. Not only will art subsidies remove resources from nonartistic pursuits, but subsidies may cause the quality of art to decline, from the perspective of consumers. John Updike wrote: "Government money in the arts, I fear, can only deflect artists from their responsibility to find an authentic market for their products, an actual audience for their performance."[11]

The economic approach stresses the notion of opportunity cost. Subsidies are a good idea only if, once all effects are taken into account, their dollar-valued benefits outweigh their dollar-valued costs.

The Federal Writers' Project of the New Deal supported Saul Bellow, Richard Wright, Ralph Ellison, and Zora Neale Hurston, among other individuals who later became noted writers (see chapter 3). Many literature lovers then conclude that the program was a good one. The economist, in contrast, could point out that the Federal Writers' Project spent $27 million for about one thousand books and pamphlets, at a cost of $27,000 per publication. Translated into dollars for the year 2000, this amounts to $337,500 per publication, or $337.5 million for the total. While some of the publications were of very high quality, they cost a great deal. It is hard to believe that offering indiscriminate literary advances of $337,500 per work is a worthwhile investment, even if it produces some first-rate books. Frederic Bastiat, writing in the nineteenth century, argued that proponents of arts subsidies typically focus on "what is seen" and neglect "what is not seen," namely the other projects and outputs that would have been funded with the money.[12]

One estimate (Wyszomirski 1999, p. 134), aimed at defending the New Deal's Works Progress Administration (WPA), suggested that the $5 million invested in the five core art projects of the WPA produced artistic outputs later worth $450 million. In reality those investments did not make overwhelming economic sense. Had the $5 million been invested in the stock market at the end of 1934, as of December 1999 (1999 is the date of publication of Wyszomirski's book), it would have yielded more than $773 million. Of course the comparison is highly sensitive to the chosen starting and ending dates, and if we picked other dates, the investment in paintings might look better. Furthermore these pictures yielded enjoyment in the interim. Nonetheless the most acclaimed arts program in U.S. history—the WPA—was not an overwhelming success in economic terms, if we compare it to alternative investments.[13]

In the economic framework, the arts should be subsidized only when they produce significant "positive externalities" at the relevant margin. A positive externality occurs to the extent that artistic production benefits individuals other than the paying customers. For instance, the arts may improve the social and moral climate of the nation or may spur more general forms of economic development. When such externalities are present, the total social value of art is greater than what people are willing to pay for in the private marketplace. A subsidy, if applied correctly, can induce more socially beneficial art and create more resources than it costs.[14]

Platitudes about the wonders of the arts do not constitute an argument for an externality at the relevant margin. The arts in general, by bringing "sweetness and light" into our lives, make the world a much better place, above and beyond what we have paid for them. This point, however, does not suffice to drive policy. The question is whether *more* art, at the margin, will do much to improve human welfare. If an arts council funds an extra show at the Whitney Museum, the rate of economic growth in New York is unlikely to increase.

In the absence of such a marginal externality, the economic approach implies that artistic production is best left to the market. Consumers will then buy just enough art until the social value from producing more art, as defined in terms of willingness to pay, would equal the social cost of producing that art. No further improvement in human welfare would be possible.

In contrast, most subsidy advocates start by asking whether art subsidies make our society more beautiful. We then can weigh whether this beauty is worth the cost in terms of efficiency, but efficiency alone does not prejudge the matter. In this view art has a value above and beyond what people are willing to pay for it. It may be better, all things considered, to have a less efficient but more beautiful society.

Many subsidy advocates go further. They conceive of policy benefits, including health, safety, and prosperity, primarily in aesthetic rather than in economic terms. They are evaluating all of society, not just arts policy, from what is primarily an aesthetic point of view. A wealthy society is presumably a precondition for a healthy society, and in that regard efficiency plays a role in supporting the aesthetic. For that reason, the typical subsidy advocate does not (or at least need not) ignore efficiency. But many subsidy advocates subordinate efficiency to the aesthetic, whereas the economist subordinates the aesthetic to the individual preferences behind the efficiency standard.

## Rapprochement?

The best-case scenario would allow for a rapprochement between the economic and aesthetic perspectives. If we examine the evidence and positive arguments with sufficient care, they might produce agreement on a number of practical questions. The remaining disagreements might be smaller and more manageable than the broader philosophic issues raised above. Through this method we might make progress on the concrete questions of arts policy.

The path here is a bit complex, and takes the following outline. First I start with some purely economic arguments for (some kinds of) subsidies, such as the economic development argument and the free-lunch argument. I will downgrade their importance, and they will not reemerge as factors to shape policy. Later parts of this chapter proceed to two issues—the decentralization argument and the prestige argument—that have force in both economic and aesthetic terms. So when using these arguments to shape policy, I hope to show that the relevant conclusions will be supported by a confluence of economic and aesthetic perspectives. We can therefore sidestep some of the stickier philosophic issues.

Once these arguments are laid out, the three following chapters will examine which institutions do the best job in light of the decentralization and prestige arguments. These chapters will cover the practical topics of direct subsidies, indirect subsidies, and copyright protection for the arts. The final chapter will tie together the philosophic and empirical investigations with some concrete policy recommendations, some remarks about the liberal state, and an account of why agreement is so hard to come by in this area.

## The Economic Development Argument

Many externalities arguments fail to establish a strong case for government subsidies. For instance subsidy advocates frequently cite the economic benefits of a healthy artistic community for a city. The arts generate employment, attract tourists, and produce tax revenue. All these effects may contribute to the general social welfare. The English composer Henry Purcell was an early proponent of arguments of this kind. In the preface to his opera *The Fairy Queen,* he claimed that opera subsidies would draw tourists and make London an economically thriving city.[15]

Insofar as the arts spur economic development, the decentralization argument, discussed further below, captures the relevant truths, at least in the American context. To anticipate that claim, the most likely positive scenario is when a private or political entrepreneur spots and invests in an undervalued artistic cluster. For this result we must look toward multiple and varied sources of financial support. No single firm, agency, or individual has proven adept at picking artistic winners across a large span of human achievement. More generally, the production of new and diverse ideas—cultural and otherwise—will contribute to economic growth. Given that we are keeping the decentralization argument on the table, we can set aside economic development as a separate concern.

More generally, the economic benefits of the arts do not themselves necessarily translate into an argument for subsidy. First, the ability of the arts to attract tourists, generate employment, and produce tax revenue implies that those arts are likely to be economically viable in their own terms. Furthermore the arts add value to a region, but a region adds value to the arts. We therefore can expect cities and the arts to come together, even in lieu of a subsidy. In the language of economics, getting the arts into cities might be a game of coordination or a question of finding a common locale. Most urban economic activity both produces and receives synergistic benefits (thus the willingness to pay higher city rents), but this does not imply that all urban activities require government subsidy.

Second, social benefits are not unique to the arts. Most productive activities bring social benefits to large numbers of people. Most kinds of economic activity create new jobs, raise the tax base, and contribute to general prosperity and social order, all of which yield positive externalities. The relevant policy question is, not whether the arts involve some positive externality, but whether the "economic development externality" from the arts is greater than from alternative investments. In fact, if the arts require subsidy to flourish, they are unlikely to be an especially strong engine of economic growth, whatever their other virtues.

*Some* activities have to be the ones that provide the greatest economic stimulus to localities, and of course this may include the arts. Nonetheless we have no firm evidence that the arts, on average, rank especially high on this list. Even if the arts stand well above the average, it is our duty, as policy analysts, to promote the *best* alternative on the menu. In contrast, the emphasis on decentralization and entrepreneurship looks for instances of undervalued resources. The arts in general need not be undervalued, but good institutions can still help us find particular instances of undervalued artistic creations.

We should be skeptical of "economic impact" studies that show the importance of the arts to a community. A study of this kind might show that an arts festival or new arts arena brings millions of dollars in economic value. But these studies typically treat arts expenditures as creating value out of nothing. Implicitly it is assumed that if the money had not been spent on the arts, no other economic or social values would have been produced. Again, the relevant comparison is whether an arts arena leads to more value than some alternative. When we look at economic impact studies for one industry at a time, they all appear to show high benefits. But this means that the net benefits of any single project are low, zero, or perhaps even negative on average. By investing in one good idea we are always forsaking another good idea. In essence those studies list gross benefits rather than net benefits. Furthermore, once an economic impact study is being done, the resources are likely no longer undervalued.[16]

To compound the inaccuracies, economic impact studies assume a "multiplier" effect. Under the multiplier hypothesis, the expenditure of a single dollar leads to a creation of several dollars' worth of value. To provide an example, the construction of an arts arena helps nearby restaurants, which in turn increases the demand for waiters, which in turn sends more money into the community, and so on. As the argument goes, the expenditure of a single dollar on the arts arena might create three or four dollars of value, once the money filters through the economy. Even if we accept the logic behind the multiplier effect, it does not demonstrate a relevant externality. Had the arts arena not been produced, the money would have stimulated some other set of demands and created some other set of multiplier effects. The *net* multiplier effect from the arts arena still might be zero or negative, unless it can be demonstrated that the arts are especially productive. No such demonstration, however, has been offered.[17]

In addition a community must invest resources to attract artistic activities from other regions. If the arts do bring net benefits, these benefits will, to some extent, be reflected in the cost of bidding for those activities. To provide a simple analogy, Silicon Valley is an economic powerhouse. Nonetheless the costs of bidding Silicon Valley into Connecticut would probably exceed the benefits.[18] Furthermore when cities court sports teams, arenas, and arts donations, often they are bidding those resources away from other cities. In this regard the gains of a single city (or country) do not always bring net gains for the world as a whole.

We do see particular cases where artistic heritage has an especially high and obvious economic value, and centralized action is required. Consider the city of Venice. It is hard to believe that Venice would have a healthier economy if it paved over its canals and turned that space over to street vendors. Venice therefore has no comparably effective way of investing the money it spends on preservation. So this is a good argument for subsidizing the historic preservation of Venice, but it does not provide a good reason to subsidize the arts more generally.

## The "Free-Lunch" Argument: Small Sums vs. Large Sums

The NEA, like many other governmental subsidies, looks best when we measure its cost in per capita terms. NEA expenditures, at their height, were no more than 65¢ for each American citizen. Currently the figure is below 50¢ a person, and it is unlikely to rise dramatically in the foreseeable future.

Some subsidy advocates talk as if subsidy programs literally cost us nothing or only a negligible sum. The economist, brought up to believe there is no free lunch, typically considers this argument absurd. Nonetheless it reemerges frequently in the intuitions of art lovers, so let us look at it more carefully, distinguishing between more and less extreme forms of the argument.

Under the more extreme argument, the taxes for the NEA literally cost us nothing, once we translate them into per capita terms. While individuals have less money to spend, the sum forgone is small. Arguably there are no major individual "life projects" that will fail to be achieved, for want of the 50¢ or even for want of a few dollars (keep in mind that most poor Americans do not pay income taxes at all). Most people have some amount of financial slack built into their plans. They die before spending all their money and do not care whether their bequest to their children is a few dollars more or less. Perhaps the small sums are never noticed one way or the other. Even in Germany, which has among the highest direct subsidies per capita of the arts, the sum falls in the range of $80 per person per year.

In contrast, government subsidies bring large and visible benefits in the form of discrete projects. The beneficiaries notice the difference, as the world receives some artworks that otherwise would not have been produced. These artworks benefit relatively small numbers of people, including the artist, but the benefits are significant for each recipient. Most of the benefits lie well above the threshold of noticeability, and thus they increase human happiness.

The less extreme form of the argument, rather than finding a free lunch, relies on antiegalitarian intuitions. We take small amounts from many individuals to give concentrated benefits to a few, and indeed often to the relatively wealthy. The distribution of goodness in society becomes less equal, but our peaks of aesthetic achievement become more beautiful. Subsidy supporters do not like to publicize this reality, but these antiegalitarian intuitions are central to many of the arguments for subsidies.

In more academic terms, the philosophical doctrine known as "perfectionism" suggests that societies should seek to reach their highest possible peaks, even if this requires a sacrifice of equality. The threshold argument and the perfectionist argument operate together to reinforce intuitions in favor of subsidies.[19]

If we accept this portrait, subsidies appear to be a good deal from the standpoint of an outside observer. In terms of real human happiness they cost either nothing or close to nothing. At the same time they create concentrated pockets of joy and aesthetic wonder. Many of the costs fall below the noticeability threshold, and many of the benefits lie above it. It is no wonder that the logic of subsidy meets with relatively little resistance from taxpayers when applied on a case-by-case basis.

We could, of course, justify many subsidies on these grounds, not just subsidies to the arts. We could tax each person a penny and redistribute the funds to a few hundred or to a few thousand people. No one would bear much of a real cost in terms of happiness, but the fund recipients could undertake new and valuable projects. A sufficiently small tax, applied to a broad enough base, will involve very small per capita costs.

The threshold and perfectionist arguments for subsidies have persuasive force, but they also prove too much. As stated above, they could justify virtually any small subsidy, provided that subsidy encouraged new projects of discrete value.

Subsidies appear less attractive when evaluated *as a bundle*. The taxes I pay for small subsidy programs do not make me worse off, even putting aside the artistic benefits I reap from the subsidies. But I am hurt by the taxation of 35 percent of my income. Much of this 35 percent is composed of very small subsidies to particular individuals, corporations, and institutions. Any one of these subsidies may make sense when evaluated individually, but they involve a real cost when evaluated as a bundle. As a bundle, they substitute governmentally determined projects for the projects *I* would have chosen.

Subsidy supporters usually prefer to present and evaluate the subsidy in stand-alone terms. Subsidy critics portray arts subsidies as part of a larger pattern of largesse and unnecessary redistribution. They see subsidies as part of a general trend to substitute political allocation for voluntary individual allocation of resources.

Similarly, subsidies appear less attractive if they are evaluated in terms of concentrated costs, not diffuse costs. For instance, it may cost, at most, a few hundred dollars of investment to protect a child, in the underdeveloped world, against a fatal or debilitating disease. For the sake of argument, let us round this number up considerably, to $2,000.[20] Under this reckoning, if we consider reallocating NEA funds to this end, NEA arts programs cost over fifty thousand lives each year. We could, in principle, abolish the NEA and distribute the funds to Haiti or India, using a private charity if we do not trust traditional mechanisms of foreign aid. Or we could abolish the NEA and every year give more than ten thousand poor Americans $10,000 each, to spend as they wish. In a later chapter, I shall refer to this as the "What about the Haitians?" critique of arts funding, and it is a challenge that any pro-subsidy view must face.

Subsidy advocates, when they compare arts expenditures to discrete alternatives, frequently have chosen examples from the military (NB: this attempt to slant the comparison has become less fashionable since 9/11). The NEA, for instance, costs us only a fraction of an aircraft carrier or a nuclear submarine. Even a simple M-1 tank costs over $3 million, which means that fewer than forty tanks would equal the NEA budget.

Which is the correct comparison to make? Do NEA subsidies cost us each less than 50¢? Do they cost thirty-five or so M-1 tanks? Or do arts subsidies cost the lives of thousands of innocent children? And should we evaluate the subsidies in stand-alone terms or as part of a larger bundle of programs?

The relevant policy alternative will depend on the political climate of the day. But we should not proceed by comparing arts subsidies to the least attractive opportunity for those funds, such as the possibility of "an extra 50¢ for everybody." To the extent we can "play God" with the government budget—the very presupposition of policy analysis—we can spend those dollars as we wish. If we accept the threshold and perfectionist arguments in the first place, we would have better options than simply leaving 50¢ in the pocket of each individual.

We started by presenting the free-lunch argument as a potential reason for arts subsidies. But it is also a potential reason *not* to have such subsidies. Under one interpretation of the choices before us, we are condemning thousands of innocent children to death and disease when we subsidize the arts.

I now consider two other arguments for government involvement in the arts, arguments that I consider to be more significant—the decentralization argument and the prestige argument.


## The Decentralization Argument


In some areas of human life, we learn by amassing the cooperation of "the best and the brightest" through centralized institutions. The Manhattan Project proceeded this way in its later stages. Or if we wish to study quarks, it may be best to invest heavily in a single, high-powered particle smasher (though not all scientists agree on the cost-effectiveness of this approach).

Other endeavors require more decentralization. Artistic discovery, for instance, is rarely a matter of brute force, or amassing enough laborers to work on perfecting a single technology. Rather we are hoping that the artist can "look at things differently" and see something that others have not. To make this happen, the artist must have the ability to market his or her vision to a diverse set of consumers, donors, and funders. It is unlikely that any single source of support will grasp the importance of all these innovations. Creativity flourishes when many different visions have a chance of succeeding.

Along these lines, we can view arts funding as a portfolio or investment problem. In most cultural markets, if we are trying to pick tomorrow's winners, we cannot forecast in advance what will work. In this regard cultural markets resemble Internet start-up firms or classic R & D problems. A few tries will hit it big, and many more will fail. In this kind of environment it makes sense to try many different approaches, rather than put all our eggs in one basket.

The American system helps generate artistic innovations, encourages new ways of marketing and distribution, and supports competing critical visions for artistic contributions. In essence, the American system satisfies the "Hayekian" standard that institutions should support the generation and dissemination of knowledge. Austrian economist Friedrich A. Hayek emphasized "competition as a discovery procedure" in many of his writings, and stressed the inability of a central authority to plan discovery. The market has the virtue of mobilizing decentralized knowledge. Entrepreneurs have opportunities to test their diverse visions in a setting with many differing sources of financial support.

Hayek's argument has often been viewed as a plea for laissez-faire, but a look at arts policy belies the necessity of that interpretation. In reality, the argument implies that we should have many decentralized sources for producing and evaluating ideas. This may or may not imply laissez-faire, depending on the institutional setting. Both tax breaks for knowledge-producing institutions and a publicly subsidized university system may encourage decentralization, to provide two examples. American arts policy uses government to induce a more decentralized pattern of financial support than would arise through pure laissez-faire.[21]

These policies do *not* imply that investments in the arts, relative to alternatives, yield especially high social returns. We should not think in terms of subsidizing the arts at the expense of other activities, or giving the arts special status. Rather we should think of American policy as encouraging decentralization for all creative activities, the arts included.

In this regard the development and decentralization arguments are distinct. The development argument asserts that the arts bring net economic advantage at the relevant margin. The decentralization approach seeks the greatest possible chance of generating, at the relevant margin, whatever brings the greatest net economic advantage.

Most deliberate governmental attempts to stimulate the discovery process have failed, and for reasons that Hayek and other economists have outlined. Government does not have the knowledge needed to centrally plan innovation. To provide one well-known example, after the energy crisis of the 1970s the U.S. government subsidized research into alternative energy sources, such as synfuels and solar energy. The end result was wasted money and little or no net technological progress with energy conservation. The government had no idea which energy-saving technologies were going to be the winners. Most improvements in energy efficiency have come from market-based institutions, encouraged by the desire to save money or to earn a profit from a new technology.

Governments usually stimulate discovery best when they eschew central planning, instead providing support according to some non-market criteria. This approach does not require that government can do an especially good job of picking winners, or that government is smarter than the market. It requires only that government distribute its support according to some principle differing from what is already available. The real question is not whether decentralization is beneficial in today's world, but rather how we should encourage decentralization at the margin.

## Why We Should Support Decentralization

At least three arguments suggest that government should, either directly or indirectly, help markets achieve a more effective degree of decentralization.

The first argument for decentralization invokes the aesthetic approach. In this view more art is desirable, especially if the new art meets high critical standards and can stand the test of time. We therefore should invest in the preconditions of quality art, namely diverse sources of financial support.

The second argument for decentralization invokes the perspective of the economist, and Paretian welfare economics in particular. Information is to some extent a public good and involves a positive externality. That is, creators do not reap the full reward of their labors.

In the nonartistic realm, the discoverers of quantum mechanics created great value but were paid relatively little. Thomas Edison was one of the wealthiest inventors in his time, but he reaped only a small fraction of the value he created. In the arts, the great creators make possible whole artistic genres and revolutions, yet they do not receive compensation for these indirect effects. Shakespeare, Mozart, and Beethoven all made a good living in their lifetime, but they did not reap anything close to the full value of their labors. Each offered lasting contributions to other artists and to the human race. Picasso was much wealthier than these creators, but still he received money only for his own paintings. He received nothing for enabling the innovations of Braque, Gris, and many other modern artists.

The greatest creators are undercompensated relative to their efforts. So if a mechanism encourages first-rate creation, it will find support from an economic perspective as well. Information is a public good with positive external benefits. Once it is produced, it typically spreads more widely than the initial creators can charge for. One estimate (Nordhaus 2004) suggests that creators receive no more than 5 percent of the value of their innovations.

Copyright does not eliminate this imperfection, even when it can be enforced. Copyright law is based on the distinction between an idea and the expression of an idea. At most it protects rights to the expression, but not to the idea itself. So copyright law can stop someone from reproducing an image of a painting, but it gives the creator nothing when others learn from his or her inspiration. Ideas remain undersupplied, even when the available artistic products make their way in the marketplace. That being said, an effective copyright regime is a good spur to decentralized creativity.

The third argument for decentralization also comes from economics. Most extant analyses suggest that entrepreneurs undersupply variety to consumers. Assume that an entrepreneur is thinking of marketing a new kind of music, say in the form of a compact disc. Buyers will value that disc from, say, a range of $2 to $40. The seller usually cannot price-discriminate perfectly and thus will pick some price in the middle, say $15. Many consumers are thus reaping more value than they must pay for. Entrepreneurs will not take these extra valuations into account when deciding to introduce new products, as they care only about what they can charge people for. Too few new products will be introduced, again by the standards of Paretian welfare economics.[22]

Note that the weight of these arguments does *not* suggest subsidies to art per se. Perhaps we have too few great creators, and too little variety. But we cannot make any direct leaps from these claims to the topic of art. Directly subsidizing more variety in art, for instance, would mean less variety in other areas. We might have less variety in foods, cars, pencils, or scientific discoveries. No argument has been made that more variety in art, or ideas in art, is more important than, say, more variety in science. For that reason, arguments two and three do not show that we should target art in any particular way. At most the arguments establish that we should encourage decentralized financial support for all creative activities, the arts included. This point will prove critical as the argument proceeds.

We see also that the two perspectives behind the decentralization argument—economic and aesthetic—offer slightly different rationales for subsidy. The critic's perspective says that decentralization has produced good art, so we should support an effective art-generating mechanism. It does not ask whether we are investing too much in decentralized support for creativity, relative to alternative uses for those resources. The economist's perspective implies we should invest more in creative discovery, relative to what a pure market would bring. It does not refer directly to art, though of course the notion of creative discovery includes art.

## The Prestige Argument

One version of the externalities argument cites national, regional, or cultural prestige. Many citizens take pride in the fact that their country produces art of a certain kind, even though they are not willing to pay for that art as customers. They like the idea that their society excels in creative activities, at least provided those creations are prestigious ones. Martin Archer Shee, writing in 1809, argued that governments should support the arts, because societies win their historical prestige through their artistic contributions; he referred to "living dignity and deathless fame."[23]

In similar fashion, many British and French citizens supported public subsidies to the Concorde in Britain and France, even though they never expected to fly in the plane. We salute flags, sing national anthems, and sometimes even fight wars, all in the name of national symbolism and prestige.

In similar fashion, we favor arts policies partly for symbolic reasons. Subsidy advocates want an art that has a link to the public sphere. They like the idea that their government has a hand in something noble. They want to be proud, not only of their country and their arts, but also of their governing body. A government that supports the arts is seen as more beautiful and more prestigious. The supporters of that state can feel good about themselves as voters and citizens. The French in particular appear to hold this motive. They will on one hand purchase American popular culture but in the political arena support trade restrictions on those same products and heavy subsidies for French art.

For this reason, it is often beside the point to argue that the arts will flourish without direct subsidies in the instrumental sense. Even if the claim is true, it does not satisfy the strong preference of many to have a state that honors creativity and backs up that honor with direct expenditures.

Furthermore many observers find something objectionable about the idea of allowing the arts to fall exclusively within the private sector. They feel that the arts should, to some degree, be brought within the push and pull of democratic discourse. These individuals want their government to make a statement that the arts are about more than simply money and about more than mere contractual agreements. They want the arts to be viewed as a vital part of a national or regional heritage, and one that receives official recognition from the government as such. Recognition of this kind requires government financial support and government arts programs. Walter Benjamin's (1986) famous essay "The Work of Art in an Age of Mechanical Reproduction" spoke of artworks as surrounded by an aura, but this phenomenon extends to the public sector as well. Government subsidies to art help produce the aura of democratic politics, especially in western Europe.

To cite another example of this principle, national parks also have an aura. Many people think it wrong that a private individual should have the control and dominion over nature that private property implies. They favor national parks, not only because they want the parks to be freely available, but also because they want the parks to be publicly owned. Publicly owned parks constitute a statement that the bounty of nature is, as a matter of right, freely available to all. In this view, the case for public ownership is not vitiated by the fact that the parks are patronized by the wealthy more than by the very poor. Rather it is simply unacceptable for one individual to invoke a private property right to exclude another individual from a more generally owned natural heritage. Government ownership of parks follows from this attitude.

Note that the prestige argument can be given an aesthetic or an economic interpretation. In the language of aesthetics, such a state and polity is nobler and more beautiful, and thus desirable for its own sake. In the language of economics and externalities, the argument for government art subsidies is that many individuals *want* government support for the arts. By subsidizing the arts, the government satisfies these urges for a particular kind of society and a particular kind of government. This kind of satisfaction, by definition, cannot be procured through private market transactions. The marketplace cannot produce "government support for the arts," no matter how well market institutions might work in the traditional economic sense.

The prestige argument also relies on a different implicit notion of subsidy than does the decentralization argument. For the decentralization argument to work, the subsidy must actually encourage the extent and diversity of creative enterprise. Many subsidies, of course, do not, as we will see below. For the prestige argument to work, the subsidy need only be seen as a subsidy in the eyes of those enjoying the prestige. It should be as visible and as public as possible. The subsidy need not do much to encourage artistic creation, provided it appears sufficiently noble (of course to some extent image and status follow from instrumental success).

We also see why subsidy advocates describe NEA expenditures in terms of per capita costs—so many cents per head—rather than comparing the money spent on the arts to the number of poor Haitian children who could have been saved. A government is more prestigious if it funds the arts from expenditures on beer and potato chips. A government that appears to fund the arts "on the backs" of starving Haitian peasants appears less noble and thus delivers an inferior result to its supporters. In this framework the value of the program is closely related to how we describe the program. To the extent that arts funding is about producing prestige, its advocates will attempt to describe it in prestigious terms. They do this not merely to lobby or to persuade others; rather the favorable description is itself part of the desired result, namely a prestigious state that we can feel good about.

## Explaining the Pattern of Government Subsidies

The prestige argument helps explain the observed *pattern* of government subsidies, which the other externality arguments cannot do. Prestige aside, arguably the most serious externalities are for electronically reproducible popular culture. The ease of unauthorized copying, even prior to online Internet file trading, means that musical artists do not reap the full reward of their labors. While the Internet may open up more opportunities than it will foreclose (see chapter 4), a market imperfection is likely to remain. Musical artists create some social benefits that they do not get paid for, and too few recordings are produced, relative to an optimum. At least in principle, a subsidy to popular music recordings could remedy this inefficiency.

High culture is less likely to confront an externality of this kind. Many forms of high culture are performed live, which makes them harder to reproduce on a mass scale. While bootlegging of live classical performances is a common practice, it has little effect on the incomes

of performers. If Maria Callas performances had not been systemati-
cally bootlegged by her fans, her income would not have been substan-
tially higher and in fact might have been lower, owing to diminished
popularity. The heavy metal group Metallica, however, did lose business to file sharing. Similarly, unauthorized copying of discs and video-
tapes appears to be a less common practice for classical than for popular music, if only because young audiences do most of the copying.
Mass markets, especially for the young, present the biggest problems
of copyright enforcement and thus the greatest potential for market
failure.

Nonetheless we see few calls for the subsidy of heavy metal music
and rap. These subsidies would yield little in the way of prestige value.
Teenagers, who are usually bent on rebellion, would not feel better to
know that their favored art forms received government subsidy. Older
partisans of high culture would reap lower and arguably *negative* prestige returns from such a policy. Few people would feel better about
their government. That is a central reason why most direct subsidies
are for high rather than popular culture.

Subsidy advocates typically favor government support for only a very
limited set of aesthetic activities. They favor subsidies to opera, art museums, and classical ballet. Some commentators have pushed the margin and called for subsidies to pop music and jazz. The Netherlands,
unlike most other western European countries, has subsidized puppet
theater and pantomime. The Japanese subsidize flower arranging. But
few individuals favor a wide extension of subsidies beyond traditional
high culture. The NEA has programs for the American folk arts, and
for jazz, but these yield prestige through mechanisms of patriotism and
political correctness.[24]

In this context we should not think of the aura of opera as somehow
"causing" government subsidies to high art. Rather, common processes
cause both the aura and the subsidies. People have supported the aura
of high art for the same reasons that they have supported government
subsidies to opera. They consider opera worthy of an aura and worthy
of a subsidy.[25]

Why do we focus subsidies on putting art *in museums*? The display of
paintings in the Bellagio casino, in Las Vegas, attracted more attention

and visitors than most traditional art exhibits. Thomas Hart Benton remarked: "If it were left to me, I wouldn't have any museums. . . . Who looks at paintings in a museum? I'd rather sell mine to saloons, bawdy houses, Kiwanis and Rotary Clubs, Chambers of Commerce—even women's clubs. People go to saloons, but never to museums." To prove the point, Benton lent his *Persephone* painting (now in the Kansas City Atkins Museum of Art) to nightclub owner Billy Rose, who displayed it in his club The Diamond Horseshoe, where forty-three thousand people saw it in three weeks. During a comparable time span, only two art museums at that time had higher attendance, and that was counting large numbers of student field trips. The nightclub exhibit, however, yielded little prestige.[26]

Subsidy advocates neglect other unwelcome implications of the externalities argument. If "good" artistic works have beneficial social consequences, most likely "bad" artistic works have negative social consequences. Not all art is elevating, ennobling, educational, or of enduring value. Many artworks are dull, stupid, socially irresponsible, or offensive. Nor would "quality" artworks escape criticism in this regard. A long tradition in philosophy, as exemplified by Plato's Socrates, argues that the most moving artworks tend to be the most dangerous and to hold the greatest appeal to the base parts of our souls. In *The Republic* Socrates speaks of "the war between philosophy and poetry" and takes the side of philosophy. Socrates raises the possibility of banning the poetry of Homer from the ideal state and teaching only those artworks that encourage virtue.

If some artworks make our society worse, the externalities argument suggests that we should discourage them. We could censor them or at least make them more costly through legal means. Once we accept the premise that the government should be involved in the arts directly, it is a short step from "good art, encourage," to "bad art, discourage." Many subsidy advocates will disavow this conclusion (note the contrast with extreme conservatives, who often favor censorship but not subsidy), but it is difficult to see why. The very case for direct subsidies requires that government can tell good art from bad with reasonable facility. Subsidy advocates presumably have discarded the premise of governmental neutrality across the arts. We need not throw rappers into the gulag, but we can imagine a variety of policies, from selective taxes to selective copyright enforcement, that would discourage "bad" art forms from competing for consumer attention. Censorship, however, is not generally conducive to prestige, at least not in twenty-first-century American liberal discourse. Proposals to control or limit bad art have not caught on.

To summarize a few of the conclusions, the prestige argument can clash with the decentralization argument. The decentralization argument calls for effective subsidies, whereas the prestige argument calls for visible subsidies. The economic version of the decentralization argument calls for general support for creativity, whereas the prestige argument calls for very particular forms of arts support. We cannot resolve these differences on a purely theoretical level, so now we turn to the history of American arts programs and arts funding. In chapter 5, armed with a better empirical sense of how things have worked, we will return to the question of what exactly should be done and why.

# 2. Indirect Subsidies:
## The Genius of the American System

American arts subsidies frequently come in disguised form, but they are effective nonetheless. The genius of the American system is to get most arts support off the direct public books. Instead it encourages competition for funds and the proliferation of the intermediate institutions that constitute civil society.

U.S. policy is based on indirect subsidies to the arts, rather than direct subsidies. Direct subsidies occur when governmental agencies write checks to artists or art institutions. An indirect subsidy arises when government policy somehow influences relative prices, or relative returns, to encourage the production of art. As we will see, "indirect" subsidies often have a more positive affect on cultural consumption than do "direct" subsidies. The word "direct" in "direct subsidy" simply means that the funds go directly to the artist or arts institution. It does not imply that good art, or its consumption, is achieved in direct fashion.

The notion of indirect subsidy is a broad one, and it conceivably covers many aspects of government policy. It could involve the enforcement of law and order, national security, economic policies that create prosperity, and the freedom of international trade, all of which tend to benefit the arts. The advocate of indirect subsidies may favor all these measures. Indeed any endorsement of indirect subsidies presumably covers "good policy" in general. Nonetheless to focus the discussion, I look at indirect subsidies that use specific mechanisms to have well-defined impacts on the arts. "Allowing American business to prosper" is perhaps our best and most important arts policy, but it is not sufficiently specific for a book of this focus.

While many commentators recognize that indirect subsidies benefit the arts, they do not regard indirect subsidies as a form of arts policy. Robert Hughes (1995), in his *Time* cover essay, equated abolishing the NEA and the Corporation for Public Broadcasting with the elimination of all federal arts policy. Edmund Wilson wrote in 1981: "We came quite late to the realisation that there may be something to the arts. A mere 15 years ago the National Endowment for the Arts was founded along with the National Endowment for the Humanities. Most state art councils are even younger." Both authors—highly intelligent and highly cultured—completely miss the importance of indirect subsidies in the American system.[1]

The distinction between direct and indirect subsidies underlies European and U.S. approaches to arts policy. Commonly a German, French, or Italian theater, museum, or orchestra will receive 80 percent or more of its budget directly from government. We are beginning to see cutbacks and exceptions. The Louvre was asked to find private funding in 1993, but this still amounts to less than a third of its operating budget. In the United States, direct government support accounts for no more than 5 percent of the total budget of nonprofit arts organizations.[2]

According to figures for U.S. symphony orchestras, 33 percent of their income comes from private donations; endowments and related sources account for another 16 percent. Concert income generates 42 percent of revenue, and direct government support provides only 6 percent. Looking at nonprofit arts institutions more generally, individual, corporate, and foundation donors make up about 45 percent of the budget. Twelve percent of income comes from foundation grants; this is two and a half times more than the contribution of the NEA and state arts councils combined. While these numbers fluctuate each year, they provide a rough measure of the relevant magnitudes.[3]

That being said, the U.S. government supports the arts far more than these figures would indicate. Let us now turn to indirect subsidies in more detail, starting with the role of the tax system. American policy provides support for artistic nonprofits but lets donors decide which institutions will receive the funds. The government is removed from the role of judging artistic quality, yet creative activity receives a spur nonetheless.

Before proceeding, note that arts lovers take more pride in direct subsidies than in indirect subsidies, and see greater recognition for the arts therein. The case for indirect subsidies thus relies on the decentralization argument, and receives less support from the prestige argument. Let us now examine this system in more detail, with an eye toward how it stimulates the decentralized discovery of creative ideas.

## Donations and the Tax System

The tax system provides the most significant arts subsidy in the United States. Rough estimates suggest that Americans donated over $29.4 billion to the category "Arts, Culture, and the Humanities" in 2003. This amounts to about $100 for each individual in the United States. In contrast, individual private philanthropy to the arts is virtually nonexistent in most European nations. If we look at individual donors, Americans give almost ten times more to nonprofits, per capita, than their French counterparts give.[4]

Approximately 60 percent of American taxpayers—most of all the wealthy—itemize their deductions. It is believed that these individuals account for the overwhelming majority of cultural donations. For these individuals, the donation of $1.00 to a nonprofit institution reduces taxes between $0.28 and $0.40, depending on the individual's tax position. Tax deductibility of individual donations dates from an act of Congress in 1917, following the introduction of the income tax in 1913.[5]

Using economic language, donations appear to exhibit "price elasticity" in the range of –0.9 to –1.4. In other words, for every $1.00 the Treasury loses from the deduction, private nonprofits receive additional donations in the range of $0.90 to $1.40. That being said, these figures supply only the local elasticities, in the range of observed variables. We do not know, for instance, how much very large changes in tax rates would affect donations and nonprofits. Nonetheless if we take this figure as a workable and available estimate, the U.S. government is making a fiscal sacrifice in the range of $26 billion to $41 billion to support the arts.[6]

Time donations—equal in scope to 390,000 full-time volunteers— are at least twice as valuable as dollar donations. As of the early 1990s, the average time donor had an income of over $56,000. That would place the implicit dollar contribution of these time donations at over $20 billion, with some estimates going as high as $25 billion. Note that the income tax encourages time donations as well as dollar donations. An extra hour spent working for one's employer is subject to tax, but an hour spent working for the arts is not. Taxes induce individuals to substitute "fun" activities of this kind in lieu of taking another job, working more hours, or starting an additional business.[7]

The estate tax also boosts arts donations. To avoid paying taxes on bequests, many individuals leave money to nonprofits and arts institutions.[8]

European governments do not offer comparable tax benefits to their arts. France, for instance, limits tax deductions to 1 percent of taxable income for individuals and 0.1 percent for corporations. Other countries, such as Germany, have allowed tax deductibility in law but made the deduction unworkable through bureaucratic restrictions. In particular, individual donors had to give through complex intermediary institutions and endure heavy paperwork. In 1999 Germany took steps to move closer to the American model, but the fundamental nature of German arts policy has yet to make the transition. France is beginning to make similar steps. England allows tax deductions but also makes the requirements more difficult than in the United States. Typically a taxpayer has had to agree to make payments for at least seven years to earn the deduction. Furthermore, the donations have not always been deductible at the top marginal rate, but rather at a lower rate.[9]

For these reasons, some European arts institutions, especially in Great Britain, find their leading private donors in the United States. In the mid-1980s, J. Paul Getty donated $62.5 million to the National Gallery in London, the largest donation the institution has received.

The Tate has raised significant American funds as well. To capture such donations, many British nonprofits now have American affiliates with tax-exempt status in the United States. Even a donation small by American standards can get an individual invited to prestigious British parties or placed on a British nonprofit board. Given the smaller scale of philanthropy in the United Kingdom, a donation of a given size brings more clout to the donor. Some European countries, such as France and Italy, hardly have private foundations at all, largely because of legal restrictions and unfavorable tax treatment.[10]

## American Foundations

Government policy has given U.S. private foundations legal and tax advantages. Foundations do not have to pay federal, state, or local taxes, and they are allowed to operate in perpetuity with very general stated objectives.

American foundations are significant in their size and scope. In 1999 American foundations gave an estimated $1.55 billion to the arts. Recent estimates put foundation assets at around $400 billion, but of course this number fluctuates with donations and asset prices.[11]

In a typical year the largest foundation arts donors are the J. Paul Getty Trust, the Lila Wallace–Readers Digest Foundation, the Mellon Foundation, and the Pew and MacArthur foundations. The foundation world tends to be moderately concentrated; a 1992 estimate has 40 percent of foundation arts funding coming from only twenty-five institutions. Getty is by far the largest arts foundation, with a $4.5 billion endowment generating $250 million yearly in spending on an art museum and an art research center.[12]

Going back in history, the Ford, Carnegie, and Mellon foundations, among others, have been instrumental in promoting high-culture enterprises, most of all museums, orchestras, and libraries. The Ford and Rockefeller foundations have certified forms of art that are less mainstream, such as modern dance, beat poetry, and the contributions of Latino and African-American artists. Small private or family foundations also give significant amounts to the arts, typically depending on the idiosyncratic wishes of the founders. Under U.S. law, it can be worthwhile to start a foundation for sums less than $1 million.

In addition to their direct grants, foundations support the arts in indirect ways. In 1998 foundations contributed $3.8 billion to higher education, which in turn has done much to help the arts, as we will discuss below.[13]

In return for favorable tax treatment, the law imposes corresponding obligations on foundations, to the benefit of the arts. Since 1969, tax-exempt nonprofit institutions must spend a certain percentage of their income each year. At first the clause required either 6 percent or the rate of return on assets, whichever was greater. In 1981 the Internal Revenue Service revised the rule and put it at 5 percent. This provision forces nonprofit foundations to invest their funds in projects and institutions.[14]

This little-known rule is a significant part of American arts policy. On average, most foundations spend 5 to 10 percent of their assets, with many foundations clustered right at the 5 percent level. The legal constraint thus appears to bind in many cases. Indeed when the legal requirement changed from 6 to 5 percent in 1981, the aggregate grant rate fell from 8 to 6 percent over the following decade. Before 1969 many foundations were little more than methods of tax evasion and storehouses for private wealth. They were explicitly marketed to donors in those terms, and 70 percent of business-linked foundations had no programs for charitable giving whatsoever. The Ford Foundation, a leading arts donor, had been set up in 1937 but did not actively make grants until the 1950s. To this day most other Western democracies do not have comparable payout requirements, and thus many of their larger foundations are sluggish and inactive. Some European countries (Belgium, Austria) *limit* the amount that foundations are allowed to pay out in a given year, requiring them to maintain their capital intact.[15]

Some analysts have argued that the required rate of foundation payout should be increased from 5 to 6 percent. Foundations have accumulated more assets than had been expected, owing largely to a booming stock market. This reform might result in at least $6 to $7 billion of additional spending from nonprofit foundations in the succeeding year. If only 2 percent of this sum went to the arts, the resulting boost in foundation spending would exceed the current budget of the NEA. When the mandated payout was originally set, the Peterson Commission had called for a payout rate of 6 to 8 percent. Many politicians felt that foundations should be required to spend themselves out of existence within twenty-five years.[16]

To the extent that foundation reserves run down, foundations may work harder for subsequent funds, which may mean more effective programs, or at least more programs in line with the desires of potential donors. Furthermore relatively young foundations may be more effective than older foundations, because of sluggishness and mission drift at the latter. So we may wish to implement policies that run down current assets rather than allow them to accumulate. Note that from 1981 to 1999, 84.5 percent of the increase in foundation assets (which rose almost threefold over that period) came from new donations and the creation of new foundations, rather than from returns on existing foundation assets.[17] "Depleting" existing foundations therefore will not spell doom for the arts. These observations do not prove that a higher payout rate is better, but some case can be made for change.

## Corporate Donors

Business giving is more decentralized than is commonly recognized. Data from the 1990s show that 47 percent of all businesses surveyed gave money to the arts, and that businesses devoted an average of 19 percent of their philanthropic budgets to the arts. The most popular grants were to symphony orchestras (15 percent), performing arts centers (13 percent), museums (12 percent), and theaters (11 percent).[18]

The data do not support the common impression that only large businesses give to the arts, and that corporate donors support only a few, highly visible projects. Three-quarters of arts spending came from smaller companies with revenues of less than $50 million. Ninety percent of that money went to local arts organizations.[19]

Corporations support the arts for favorable publicity, to promote their public image, and sometimes because managers are willing to

spend shareholder funds to promote their own interests. Corporate donations have come with increasing frequency from the public relations
budgets of corporations, and for large corporations, advertising expenditures provide a good predictor of arts support. That is, companies that
advertise heavily tend to support the arts as well. A thirty-second network television advertisement can cost more than half a million dollars
during prime time. In comparison, donating a few million dollars to
the arts is relatively cheap, and raises the company's image with the
wealthy and the educated.[20]

Companies also give to the arts to extend their influence in politics
or to lower their chances of becoming political victims. Generous corporations are frequently in "negative-publicity" industries such as ciga-
rettes, air pollutants, or energy production and distribution. Philip
Morris has coined the slogan, not meant ironically, "It takes art to
make a company great." The threat of pending regulation and lawsuits
against these firms serves as an implicit subsidy to artistic nonprofits.[21]

Corporate giving, like private and foundation giving, has been influenced by public policy decisions. Corporations have received tax
breaks for supporting the arts since 1936. As with individuals, the evidence suggests that corporations give more to the arts when they receive
tax benefits for doing so.[22]

Many other tax benefits for the arts are piecemeal in nature. As a
result they are not easily described or measured.

For instance artistic institutions benefit from numerous local tax
breaks, often under the guise of urban renewal. Entrepreneurs can put together packages of direct and indirect subsidies, drawing on a wide variety
of sources. Consider the Minneapolis Artspace group, which wanted to
renovate a decrepit warehouse and turn it into artists' apartments and studios. They started by going to the State Housing Finance Agency and ap-
plying for low-income tax credits, available for renovation projects. These
credits are paid for by the federal government but allocated through state
governments. The project had an estimated value of $20 million, which
meant that the available tax credit was about $900,000 per year. This sum
is paid out yearly for ten years, or $9 million in total. ArtSpace used these
tax credits to get a bank loan of $7 million and then set up a corporate
partnership, in essence "selling" the tax credits to the corporate partner

for cash. ArtSpace also financed 20 percent of the $20 million cost from the historic tax credits available through the Department of the Interior, again "selling" these tax credits for 93¢ on the dollar. Eleven million of the $20 million total was now in hand, and construction could begin. County and state tax programs served to complete the financing, and the remainder was raised from private foundations, again with an implicit tax break for the donations.[23]

## Nonprofit and For-profit Sectors

Subsidies to artistic nonprofits benefit the for-profit sector as well. For instance Hollywood draws on stories and ideas emanating from nonprofits. *Driving Miss Daisy, Gin Game, On Golden Pond, Children of a Lesser God, Glengarry Glen Ross*, and *Prelude to a Kiss* all started as nonprofit theater before they were made into movies. Over the past twenty years, 44 percent of the new plays produced on for-profit Broadway originated in the nonprofit sector.[24]

The Beatles stand among the most popular musical groups of the last fifty years. Yet their electronic collage ideas—central to their seminal *Sgt. Pepper* album—were drawn from John Cage and German composer Karlheinz Stockhausen. Both of these figures benefited significantly from government subsidies in their careers. Stockhausen also helped inspire the genre known as "Krautrock," consisting of (nonsubsidized) German groups such as Can, Faust, and Kraftwerk. These groups subsequently exerted a strong influence on American popular music and were an early inspiration for industrial, techno, dance, and ambient music, all vibrant commercial forms. Sonic Youth, a leading "alternative" rock band, has drawn on Glenn Branca and also the "microtonal" movement. Both trends have found significant support in (subsidized) American universities.

The connections between the for-profit and the nonprofit sectors are numerous, though often difficult to trace. Nonprofit museums may inspire for-profit artists and provide them with new ideas. Galleries and dealers boost the careers and reputations of their artists by helping to place their works in nonprofit museums. American Pop Art drew on commercial illustration; commercial art and design responded in kind by turning "high culture" ideas back into popular form. When we look at the outputs of the contemporary visual arts, we cannot draw a clear line between the for-profit and the nonprofit sectors.

The literary world blurs the nonprofit and for-profit sectors as well. Public libraries and university libraries put books in the hands of readers and boost the reputations of commercial authors. They promote the idea that reading is fun. Libraries also provide a steady demand for low-selling works. This makes it easier for authors to market their ideas to publishers, provides modest royalty support, and gives authors a later chance to hit it big. In fiscal year 2002, U.S. libraries had budgets of over $8 billion, most of which came from government support, usually at the local level. This is the largest and best-developed public library system in the world.[25]

We should not think of the nonprofit and for-profit sectors as fully separate. Too frequently commentators paint a picture of one subsidized sector and another capitalist sector. But in reality popular culture often draws on government-subsidized high culture for its "research and development" efforts. Indirect subsidies to the arts have made American popular culture much stronger.

## Direct versus Indirect Subsidies

Tax subsidies allow government to support the arts while avoiding judgments about artistic merit. Any deduction to a nonprofit qualifies as a deduction for the taxpaying donor. The government need not decide what qualifies as art, or as good art, since donations to other nonprofit institutions—such as charities and churches—receive comparable tax treatment. This arm's-length relationship, however, means that tax deductions are a blunt instrument for favoring the arts. In the United States, the arts account for only about 2 percent of donations. A decision to favor the arts through the tax system means a decision to favor religion, charity, and other nonprofit causes as well. The very neutrality of the tax deduction—one of its prime advantages—means that policy does not target any specific destination for the donations. The American tax system thus favors decentralization of nonprofit activities, rather than any particular conception of art, or even any particular conception of what a nonprofit should do.[26]

In principle, the government could set standards for demarcating artistic institutions from other nonprofits. Such a policy, however, would set a dangerous precedent by having government define art. The legal definition of a nonprofit institution is fairly clear, but there are no comparable principles for defining an artistic institution. If forced to stipulate such a definition, it is unlikely that the government could avoid making detailed decisions about what should count as art, or about which arts are worth supporting. For the foreseeable future, the tax deduction to the arts will be, and probably should be, tethered to the tax deduction for other nonprofits.[27]

This very general form of subsidy does not imply complete neutrality across different visions of the arts. A decentralized system inevitably favors some artistic visions over others, whether intentionally or not. Most generally, American tax policy favors "artistic projects that can earn niches in a decentralized world." Favoring these kinds of projects represents an implicit aesthetic choice, though it is not typically seen as such. For purposes of contrast, consider the arts policies of the former Soviet Union, which included subsidy, censorship, and propaganda. This artistic environment encouraged disguised political satire, a centralist architecture of monuments and wartime memorials, and the preservation of historic performance styles, such as romantic pianism, through induced cultural and economic stasis. Overall culture declined, compared with the riches of Czarist times, but some outputs were splendid nonetheless. Furthermore many of these outputs would not have resulted from more decentralized environments. By opting for decentralization, we have lessened the chance of creating similar achievements in America and opted for other styles instead. We have favored jazz, modern architecture, Abstract Expressionist painting, and the Hollywood action movie, among other forms.

If we are willing to tolerate or perhaps welcome such nonneutralities, American tax policy has a strong record for the arts. The American success in popular culture is well known, but America's role as high-culture leader in the postwar era is less commonly recognized. Although America started from a poor high-culture base in the nineteenth century, it has become a leader in abstract art, contemporary classical composition, avant-garde fiction and poetry, and modern dance, to name just a few fields of many. Artistic nonprofits and the American tax system have supported these endeavors.

Religion and the housing market provide two analogous cases where indirect subsidies have proven effective and outperformed direct subsidies. The United States government supports religion by granting churches tax-exempt status and by making church donations tax-deductible. The government provides no direct grants of cash and gives relatively wide latitude in its recognition of legal church status. Under this regime, American churches are highly competitive, they provide enormous variety, they are wealthy, and they touch the lives of most Americans.

European churches, most of which receive direct grants from the state, tend to be sluggish and bureaucratic. European religion also - exhibits less diversity, as most countries have a small number of established churches. Turkish Moslems in Germany or Algerian Moslems in France, both of whom number in the millions, do not receive state support for their mosques. European governments must draw up lists of approved religions when deciding how to allocate funds. And despite their privileged status, European churches end up receiving less financial support than American churches do. Public-sector support, at a high enough level, tends to displace private support.

Religion does not provide an exact analogy to the arts, and the U.S. system of tax exemptions may be as much a symptom of religious success as a cause. Perhaps America can fund its churches through tax exemptions because religion is so popular in the first place. Relative to most western Europeans, Americans seem to have a special attachment to organized religion. Religion nonetheless illustrates the virtues of the indirect funding model.

The religion example also deflates some of the rationales for direct subsidies. It is frequently argued, either implicitly or explicitly, that the arts should receive direct governmental support because they are so important, noble, or sacred. Yet the religion example suggests that the very significance of an activity may make it unsuited for direct governmental support and better suited for indirect support.

The housing market is another case where tax subsidies have outperformed direct government funding. The U.S. government has made mortgage interest tax-deductible to encourage middle-class home ownership. The pros and cons of this policy goal can be debated (is home ownership really good per se?), but if we accept the desirability of increased home ownership as given, the policy has succeeded. This tax subsidy has boosted owner-occupied housing and has extended benefits to all home owners on a relatively impartial basis, while avoiding high administrative costs.

A home owner's equivalent of the NEA, which would solicit applications and pick out worthy projects for direct cash grants, would have been another option. Indeed the Department of Housing and Urban Development (HUD) has instituted policies of this general nature, but usually with poor results. Government housing programs have, for the most part, failed to achieve their stated ends and have produced waste, corruption, and government favoritism. By almost any account, HUD has been one of the least successful government agencies.[28]

Now consider a realm—namely *nature*—where *direct* subsidies often work better. Much ink has been split over the difference between nature and culture, but as a first approximation consider culture as the aesthetic beauty produced by human beings and nature as the beauty prior to human involvement (admittedly many "natural" wonders have been shaped by man, and so on).

Governments directly subsidize natural beauty, usually in the form of publicly owned and protected national parks. Governments also restrict economic development, sometimes with the motive of protecting beauty, such as when they forbid the posting of billboards near the Grand Canyon.

When preserving nature, we often wish to achieve a well-specified aesthetic outcome, such as "preservation of the Grand Canyon in its natural state." The citizenry holds a strong consensus in favor of this end, however imperfectly it may be achieved. We have seen debates about ambient pollution and helicopter flights, but for the most part we know how the Grand Canyon ought to look. There is no talk of re-designing it to have more terraces, or of painting parts of it purple. There is less need for a multiplicity of visions about the future of the Grand Canyon and thus less need for decentralization.

Contemporary art does not generate a similar visual consensus. *Ex ante* we do not know exactly how a given painting or sculpture should look (historical monuments are a potential exception, and indeed there we see more direct government involvement). It therefore makes sense for our government to limit its direct involvement. Decentralized incentives for production, which may include indirect subsidies, leave decisions about quality to consumers and donors in a competitive marketplace.

Direct government subsidies, in the realm of natural beauty, avoid another disadvantage of direct art subsidies. Return to the point that culture is produced by human beings whereas nature is not. Cultural subsidies induce artists to court politicians and bureaucrats, often by altering the content of their work. In contrast, there is no corresponding danger that "nature will pander to politicians." We would, however, fear a system that did no more than give tax breaks to private institutions taking care of the Grand Canyon. Such a policy would not ensure that the canyon remained free of billboards and advertising.

We can find other illustrative examples of how direct policy works. Consider the supply of drinking water. We have a clear and well-defined idea of what good drinking water consists of. Government suppliers can aim at this standard without undue controversy or difficulty. The costs of governmental water supply are therefore relatively low, as we do not forgo much innovation; this is one reason why government water provision is so common. Even if a privatized water supply might be better, governmental water provision has not proven disastrous in the United States or western Europe.

In contrast, governmental supply of high fashion would not run so smoothly. Many people do not agree on what a good dress looks like. Dressmakers innovate frequently and make great efforts to shape taste. Government provision likely would be a disaster. The government cannot decide easily which dresses should be produced. If the government were to have some involvement in fashion, we might subsidize the research and development stage or provide tax credits for dress purchases. But the government should not be expected to pick out the best dresses and fund them.

When the government runs an art museum of Old Masters, it is engaged in an enterprise similar to the supply of water. As with good water, there is relatively little disagreement about the great art of the past. No one questions that the National Gallery of Art displays da Vinci, Raphael, Rubens, Rembrandt, Cézanne, Monet, and van Gogh, even if not everyone likes these particular artists. For this reason, many of the most impressive artistic successes of democratic governments have focused on preserving our artistic heritage. Especially in Europe, museums, classic theater companies, and performances of classical music owe much to government funding. In most of these areas, the potentially conservative nature of government is less of a handicap. Direct government ownership and control create the least problems when there is relative unanimity of opinion about quality.

Preservation of past classics also involves a smaller danger of politicization. Choosing whether or not to include paintings by Paul Gauguin, an anarchist, in a government museum is a less controversial decision than deciding whether or not to fund current anarchist video art. Historical radicals are, to some extent, sanctioned and defused by the passage of time.

We thus see one reason why the U.S. government has provided fewer direct subsidies than European governments. European nations are more likely to have a common core of high culture that defines their national background. The Germans do not quibble over subsidizing performances of Bach, given his centrality to their history and culture. The American citizenry, more ethnically diverse in nature, and less connected to historical high culture, cannot target direct subsidies with equal facility.

## Research and Development

The two subsidized institutions that will most benefit the arts in the immediate future—the computer and the Internet—received their subsidies from the Department of Defense, not the NEA. The National Science Foundation ran the Internet in its early years. The World Wide Web was developed at CERN, the European Organization for Nuclear Research, heavily subsidized by a consortium of European governments. Many of the institutions that run Internet servers are nonprofits, universities, or otherwise subsidized by governments at various levels.

The free-for-all R & D environment of DARPA (Defense Advanced Research Projects Agency) came from the influence of Neil McElroy, secretary of defense under Eisenhower. McElroy had no military background but rather had been chief executive at Proctor & Gamble. He believed the company had succeeded by giving its R & D department free rein, and sought to replicate a similar environment for government research. Scientists used Defense Department funds to develop an early version of the Internet, originally designed to be a communications network secure against a nuclear attack. Similarly, the public university system was not designed to employ artists and musicians, although it has ended up serving that purpose. Thomas C. Schelling has coined the propitious phrase "Research by Accident."[29]

Government policies can work by creating variations in the basic environment of rewards. These variations allow some talented people to seize opportunities that otherwise would not have existed. These new incentives will have bad effects in many cases, perhaps even in the typical case. Frequently individuals exploit the variations for selfish ends with no additional social value. For instance we observe widespread waste and shirking in both the Defense Department and in universities. The federal government spends about $80 billion a year on research and development, most of which yields nothing. But in a few cases—the extreme right-hand tail of the distribution curve—the variations will support significant creative projects. At the cost of massive governmental waste we get a few occasional large R & D winners, such as the Internet and the computer. In the context of the university and the arts, we get Roy Lichtenstein and Georgia O'Keeffe, both of whom relied on public university support early in their careers.[30]

Think of the underlying logic in these terms. The world contains a large number of would-be artists, some potential winners or geniuses. Those artists will have a difficult time succeeding, but they need only a small number of "breaks" to enter the market and capture the attention of potential customers or donors. No single institution will be able to spot more than a small number of winners, due to limited resources and the intrinsic difficulty of the task. If, however, there are many different mechanisms for identifying winners and giving them breaks, a greater number of excellent creators will be identified and helped. Government funding, at its best, increases the number of mechanisms for skimming the pool of talent. The greater the diversity of funding sources, the greater the likelihood that excellent creators will find support.

This defense of decentralization does *not* mean that subsidy successes are replicable by copying past successes. In fact I hold the contrary presumption. The next governmental success story is one that we cannot yet imagine, just as the Internet was a surprise at the time. Identifying the winners *ex post* does not mean we can choose them *ex ante*. At most, the Internet example suggests that societies should have many diverse sources of financial support, including governmental ones. It does not mean that any particular source should receive more money. To make the point concrete, it is unlikely that boosting the current budget for "postnuclear planning" will lead to another development comparable to the Internet. So we do not know exactly what to do, except to opt for a high degree of financial decentralization.

## Integration and Separation

The indirect subsidies for the arts extend far beyond the tax system. Many of the most important indirect subsidies have opened up lines of trade, communications, and transport.

Since the 1920s, U.S. foreign policy has ensured that foreign markets stay open to Hollywood exports. In 1926 the Department of Commerce added a Motion Picture Section. After the Second World War, America used foreign aid and its military muscle to discourage European cultural protectionism, especially in Italy, France, and England. The struggle continued through institutions associated with the General Agreement on Tariffs and Trade and then the World Trade Organization. The

State Department also supported the cartelization of Hollywood export efforts through the major studios. Hollywood currently receives export tax subsidies, which of course support the production of films at home.

Note that this support has involved an implicit trading of favors. Hollywood might not have received governmental assistance in opening markets had it not strongly supported the American role in World War II. The major Hollywood studios continue to court politicians, in part because the studios receive political support for their export efforts; foreign box office now accounts for about half of Hollywood gross screen revenue.[31]

Some trade subsidies arise through the *failure* to enforce laws. The U.S. government has helped make America a center of the art world by relatively laissez-faire importation policies. Imported artworks, unlike most other forms of commerce, are exempt from import and export duties in the United States. This policy has stimulated American art collecting and has helped make New York a center of the art world. Note that in 1883 American artists lobbied successfully for a heavy tax on the importation of artworks, fearing competition from European creators. The famous Armory Show of 1913 introduced modern art to the United States and stimulated an entire generation of painters. The show became possible only when this tax was repealed shortly before its staging.[32]

In the areas of antiquities and ethnographic arts, until recently the U.S. government has paid little heed to stolen or smuggled items. It is commonly believed that the antiquities collection at the Metropolitan Museum of Art is founded largely on gray- and black-market transactions. One estimate places the size of the international trade in stolen or smuggled artworks at about $1 billion yearly. The United States does restrict the importation of large artistic objects from historic pre-Hispanic sites in Latin America. These restrictions have had little effect, given the ease of smuggling items through Customs. But now the Cultural Property Advisory Committee (in the State Department) is stepping up its enforcement efforts, so it remains to be seen whether this earlier, more liberal regime will persist.[33]

Other indirect subsidies have targeted the transport of goods and services within the country. The U.S. government has subsidized postal mailings since the beginning of the Postal Service in the late eighteenth century. Newspapers, which carried literary installments and informed the public about the arts, received especially favorable treatment. Starting in 1851 the Postal Service offered subsidized rates to book mailings. The period 1874 to 1885 brought further rate changes that gave a huge boost to the mailing of magazines. By the end of this time magazines were cheaper to mail than were advertising circulars. The result was a magazine boom, which gave writers a new way to reach audiences and make a living. Between 1885 and 1900, the number of magazines with 100,000 circulation or more rose from 21 to 85; by 1905 the figure was 159. By 1903 *Ladies' Home Journal* had garnered more than one million subscribers.[34]

Most generally, U.S. policies toward mass communications have generally been more supportive than European approaches. European governments, rather than aiding newspapers, typically have tried to tax them. At least since the Stamp Act crisis of 1765, Americans have parted company with the Old World suspicion of newspapers and mass media.

Radio provides another example of the greater European wariness toward mass communications. Great Britain, to this day, resorts to a radio and television tax. Circa 2003 the television tax was levied at £116 a year (almost $200) and rising.[35] U.S. policy, in contrast, welcomed radio from the beginning. During World War I, for instance, the federal government worried that private companies were not producing enough radios. The navy removed all patent restrictions on radio production, assumed all patent liability, and set uniform standards for radio manufacture. The production of radios boomed. It is no surprise that America was the world leader in developing radio programs, and using radio as a means to communicate culture to broad audiences.[36]

It is unclear whether the allocation of the electromagnetic spectrum counts as a subsidy to the arts. The U.S. government has distributed rights to this spectrum to commercial broadcasters for free; according to some estimates the spectrum rights would be worth at least $100 billion. Other arts subsidies would pale in comparison to this figure. But most likely this is a subsidy *to the broadcast companies* rather than a subsidy to the arts. At the margin the arts are no more profitable than before. For better or worse, the U.S. government has $100 billion less, and the broadcasters have $100 billion more. It is difficult to argue, however, that the nature and quantity of programming would be different had these rights been auctioned off. The companies still would offer those programs most likely to make money.[37]

Other indirect arts subsidies have lowered the costs of transporting individuals to and from artistic events. A culture of individual mobility will bring wider audiences to the arts, and give artists a greater number of sources of support.

In the nineteenth century the American government subsidized canal and railroad construction. The railroads proved of central importance to touring musicians, theater companies, vaudeville, and other mobile forms of culture and entertainment. Airplanes received significant government largesse during the formative years of flight. The development of commercial airliners, as we know them, was hastened by military subsidies. Since that time the ability to fly has given performers access to markets all around the United States. Airplanes also have made it easier for Americans to enjoy foreign cultures or bring back inspiration for their own productions. In the 1970s airline deregulation lowered the cost of flying. Americans are now more likely to take a flight to see an opera, or visit a museum exhibit, than before.

Water subsidies have allowed Americans to settle California and the Southwest in large numbers, thus supporting new regional cultures. This policy is not a subsidy to the arts in any formal sense, but the net result has been greater geographic diversity in American creativity.

In some exceptional cases our government has subsidized separation rather than integration. The federal government supports Native American or Indian arts by allowing tribes to maintain separate sovereignty, thus keeping Indian cultures relatively intact. Since the nineteenth century, the policy debate has alternated between desires for integration and separation. The separationists have triumphed, as reflected by the official legal status enjoyed by many Indian tribes. American Indians can grow up in a legal environment of their choosing, and they can self-identify as Indians in a formal sense. Casino gambling on reservations has provided a further boost to Native American arts, by maintaining the economic viability of those communities. These casinos are so profitable in part because American governments outlaw casinos in so many other locales.[38]

## Religion: Culture in Our Churches

Indirect subsidies to religion, discussed above, also serve as indirect subsidies to the arts. It would be a stretch to equate religion and art, but religion is one kind of aesthetic experience. Many individuals find prayer and religious participation to be intensely moving and beautiful.

The Bible and the Koran, apart from their religious significance, are among the best literary works of their respective cultures. The tax break for churches, synagogues, and mosques thus has served as an effective "Great Books" program. Many millions of Americans have close acquaintance with these texts, largely because of the strength of religion in this country. More generally, religions have spurred cultural successes in literature, music, and the visual arts.

Religious institutions house concerts in their buildings, organize choral groups, and incorporate music—often of very high quality—directly into the services. The classic chorales and masses continue to be performed in today's churches. African-American gospel music, a notable art form, arose in churches. Gospel formed a basis for later developments in soul, rhythm and blues, and rock and roll. Most of the leading Motown performers, for instance, had their earliest musical training in gospel, as did Aretha Franklin and James Brown as well. Synagogues support music from both classic and folk styles. Koranic chanting is a beautiful art form, integrating aspects of music and rhythmic speech.[39]

Finally, many religious buildings are first-rate works of architecture. The building, the pews, the hangings, and the stained glass all may contribute to this aesthetic merit. The new Catholic Cathedral in Los Angeles, the Crystal Cathedral in Garden Grove, California, and the Baha'i House of Worship in Wilmette, Illinois, are just a few of the notable religious buildings in the United Sates. Again, these structures received a significant financial boost from U.S. policy toward religions and nonprofit organizations.[40]

## Government as Publicity Agent

Government publicity helps the careers of many artists. The White House awards a Presidential Medal in the Arts, to both artists and patrons. The prize pays no money, but the associated news coverage boosts the creators' value in the marketplace and encourages patrons to give to the arts.

NEA funding, by stimulating attacks, has generated unintentional publicity for controversial artists. Andres Serrano, creator of *Piss Christ*, a polychrome photo of a crucifix submersed in urine, was only moderately well known before he became the center of a national controversy. He had received some good reviews, but it was not obvious that he could earn a living as an artist. Circa 2003 a *Piss Christ* sells for about $90,000, and Serrano's name is well known throughout the artistic community and even among the educated general public.

The 1999 Rudolf Giuliani controversy over New York City funding for the Brooklyn Museum had a similar effect. The paintings of Chris Ofili received heavy criticism, largely because the artist had used elephant dung for his portrait of the Virgin Mary. The prices for his works rose quickly, and museums competed to buy them. Lines to see the show were suddenly long. Public attention is the only thing harder for artists to get than money. The critics of government funding deliver this precious service to a select few artists who offend the sensibilities of others.[41]

## Government Jobs

The very existence of government jobs subsidizes the arts. Even in the best of times, most writers find it difficult to make a living from book sales alone. Many accept government jobs, hoping they will have time to pursue their own projects. Bureaucracy, despite its deadening effects, stimulates creativity by creating a realm of personal freedom for many employees.

William Faulkner worked for a time as postmaster at the University of Mississippi postal station. He called his section of the post office the "reading room." Nathaniel Hawthorne worked in a customshouse, after failing to get a postmaster job. Walt Whitman revised his *Leaves of Grass* while working for the Department of the Interior, although his superior fired him because he regarded the book as immoral. Herman Melville worked in a customshouse as well, although not at the time of his greatest literary productivity. William Charvat estimated that between 1800 and 1875, 60 to 75 percent of American male writers "who even approached professionalism either held public office or tried to get it."[42]

The role of government jobs is no less prominent in the history of literature more generally. Chaucer was a career public servant, Dante pursued politics, Goethe was a bureaucrat for much of his life, and Anthony Trollope held a job in the postal service, during which time he wrote most of his sixty novels. William Wordsworth, Daniel Defoe, and the Roman poet Horace worked as tax collectors. Jonathan Swift was clergy in a tax-supported church. Stendahl worked in the Napoleonic bureaucracy. In the social sciences, Adam Smith worked in a customshouse, and Edward Gibbon was a member of Parliament and lord of trade.[43]

It is a moot point whether we should count prison as a government "job," but many notable literary works have been written in enforced confinement, most notably Cervantes's *Don Quixote* and de Sade's *120 Days of Sodom*. Prison literature has been a growing genre in the United States since at least the 1960s. A longer list of incarcerated writers includes Boethius, Villon, Thomas More, Campanella, Walter Raleigh, Donne, Richard Lovelace, Bunyan, Defoe, Voltaire, Diderot, Thoreau, Melville, Leigh Hunt, Oscar Wilde, Jack London, Maxim Gorky, Genet, O. Henry, Robert Lowell, Brendan Behan, Chernyeshevsky, Dostoyevsky, and Solzhenitsyn.[44]

Today the Department of Justice and various state and local authorities support prison programs in the arts, for America's more than two million inmates. In addition to prison literature, prison art has been successful within the "Outsider" art movement. In recent times, however, prison arts programs have been curtailed. Prison authorities are worried about security issues, since most artistic tools can be turned into weapons. For that reason, most prison sculptures are now made with soap, bread, and toilet paper, none of which make effective weapons. These programs cover several million individuals, and thus form a large part of government arts policy. That being said, the programs have not brought many obvious artistic successes.[45]

State-run mental hospitals have managed some of America's most talented painters, especially in the realm of "Outsider" art. Many of these individuals flourished artistically when they were given materials and a tolerant environment. (Austria and Switzerland have gone far beyond the United States in this regard, and tend to have the best asylum artists.) Asylum stay, whatever its drawbacks, relieves creators of the need to hold down a full-time job. At its peak, in the 1960s, the American mental health system kept 559,000 persons in hospitals.[46]

The career of Martin Ramirez (1895–1963), one of America's most renowned Outsider artists, illustrates the conflicting record of the American state in this area. Ramirez created his major works while confined to the De Witt State Mental Hospital in Auburn, Alabama. The hospital had a policy of destroying the artistic works of the inmates on a daily basis. Ramirez's work survived only because he managed to hide some of his creations under his bed, and later because he found one psychologist who encouraged him and allowed him to keep working without hindrance. Later, the first exhibit of Ramirez's work was arranged at Sacramento State College; today his work is held in many major museums, including the Guggenheim, and held in high regard.[47]

## Arts in the American University

The American university system is an underappreciated vehicle for government support of the arts. By subsidizing universities, federal and state governments provide employment for painters, writers, musicians, and other creative artists. Universities also run cultural facilities, organize concerts, and spread cultural education as well.

The first American university to employ a noted artist was Columbia University, which employed composer Edward MacDowell to be chairman of the Department of Music in 1896. MacDowell remained until 1904, when he quit in protest, alleging that the university president had interfered in departmental affairs. The first artist-in-residence in an American university was American painter John Steuart Curry, who worked at the University of Wisconsin in the 1930s. The pianist Gunnar Johansen joined him there in 1939. Robert Frost received support from the University of Michigan, which in fact offered him a stipend for life. For the most part, however, the artist at the university is a post–World War II development, most of all from the 1960s.[48]

The career of Roy Lichtenstein benefited greatly from American universities. Before his commercial success as a painter, Lichtenstein taught art at SUNY Oswego, in upper New York State. At that time he had not yet developed his signature style of Pop Art, but worked in a mode closer to Abstract Expressionism. Lichtenstein then moved to Douglass College, the sister school to Rutgers University, the state university in New Jersey. He spent 1960–1963 at Douglass, where he was exposed to avant-garde influences and the so-called "Fluxus" group, which had strong roots at Rutgers. During this time Lichtenstein developed his signature style. After reaching commercial success, he left his teaching post for good. Sculptor George Segal also relied on Rutgers for financial support and the opportunity to develop his style. David Hockney taught at UCLA for part of the formative part of his career.[49]

Georgia O'Keeffe developed her style while working at West Texas State University in the early years of her career. Clifford Styll taught at Washington State University in Pullman from 1933 to 1941, during which time he had his first professional exhibit. Skeptics sometimes ask, "Where are the great artists in today's universities?" As worded, this query neglects how artists have used universities as a springboard to the commercial market.[50]

Creative writing programs, often at state or state-subsidized universities, train American writers or help them connect with publishing houses. John Barth spent the first twenty years of his career at two state universities, Penn State and SUNY Buffalo. A study of the *New York Times Book Review* found that 31 percent of the reviewed authors earned their living from the academic world (although this figure includes nonfiction books as well).[51]

Universities support the arts in many ways, not just through full-time faculty hires. In the world of classical music, almost every composer serves as a "guest composer" at a university for some period of time. Universities also are a venue for classical music performances. They bring performers to audiences, including to smaller towns such as Ann Arbor, Michigan, and Bloomington, Indiana. The recent boom in "world music" is due, in part, to the concerts held at universities. The University of California at Davis alone spends $7 million a year on the performing arts.[52]

Roughly two dozen universities are currently active in commissioning new artworks. The list includes Ohio State University, the University of Iowa, the University of Michigan, and the University of California, all state schools. The University of Iowa is arguably the leader in this regard, having commissioned more than eighty works since 1986. It put up $500,000 to sponsor a new production by the Joffrey Ballet.[53]

Hollywood relies on film schools, including the film school at UCLA—a state university—to train and recruit future directors. Hong Kong action director Tsui Hark learned some of his craft at the University of Texas. Much of the American avant-garde theater is based in drama workshops at colleges and universities. Architects rely heavily on universities for their basic training, as do many individuals in music technology and production.

The university poetry anthology—required reading for many introductory survey classes—provides the primary market demand for the writings of poets. Contemporary poets receive royalty income and some measure of fame from these volumes. Universities also subsidize many literary magazines. DePaul University has published *Poetry East*, and Southern Methodist University has published *Southwest Review*.

University presses publish many works, including fiction, that commercial houses reject. Some of these books have won great honors. John Kennedy Toole's *Confederacy of Dunces* was picked up by

Louisiana State University Press after being rejected by numerous commercial publishers. The book won a Pulitzer Prize, is now considered a classic, and sells a hundred thousand copies annually.[54]

The College Art Association lists over seven hundred art museums at American colleges and universities. Yale, Chicago, Berkeley, Michigan, Howard University, Bob Jones University, and Williams College are among those with the best-known collections, but many smaller institutions fill important niches. They cover areas—such as ethnography, ceramics, or prints—that get crowded out of many larger, nonuniversity museums. They also show many local artists, or artists in special genres, who otherwise might not receive exhibition space.[55]

College radio stations, and the college tour circuit, are critical to the success of independent rock bands and do much to help musical diversity. A commercial radio station, for instance, might play only five hundred or so songs a year. WHRB-FM, at Harvard University, estimates that it plays seventy thousand to ninety thousand songs a year. College stations offer disk jockeys far more independence, and have far more freedom from the demands of commercial advertisers. More generally, colleges and universities are central to the dissemination of new musical trends.[56]

Universities subsidize popular culture by bringing large numbers of young people together. Alternative rock, "Beat" poetry, and avant-garde movies have relied heavily on university students for base support. The university provides a natural venue for young individuals to receive and spread information about art forms, and for the formation of fads. Individuals who work typically have less time to devote to culture and are less plugged in to recent cultural trends, compared to university students. The dormitory is a natural incubator for contemporary culture and the spread of trends.

## The Nature of Educational Subsidies

Charitable donations drove the first great wave of growth of American universities at the end of the nineteenth century. The number of professors rose almost tenfold from 1870 to 1920. Federal and state governments led the second wave of growth after the Second World War. The federal government sought military and ideological benefits, whereas state governments confronted growing demands for public higher education. Until this century, most American students were enrolled in private institutions of higher education. State universities continued to grow throughout the twentieth century, however, and enrollments reached parity by 1951. Today the public sector accounts for about 78 percent of enrolled students in higher education.[57]

Subsidies to higher education remain significant. In 1995, the United States had over 14 million students enrolled in higher education and approximately 915,000 faculty, spread out over 3,706 institutions. Private schools receive large subsidies; federal direct subsidies to higher education cost $11 billion yearly, with another $18 billion allocated to research support, mostly going to private schools. Federal support alone (not including student loans) accounts for about 14 percent of higher education expenditures. Henry Rosovsky (1990, p. 262) estimates that 20 percent of Harvard's budget comes directly from government funds.[58]

If we take the public and private sectors together, National Science Foundation figures from 1995 indicate a total income for "research universities" at slightly over $87 billion. Sixteen billion of this total comes from state and local government appropriations, and $12 billion comes from federal grants and contracts, for slightly less than a third of the total.[59]

Tuition revenue relies heavily on federal and state subsidies. In 2000 federal direct and federally guaranteed loans amounted to about $41 billion, covering more than six million students Much of this student aid dates from the 1972 Education Amendments. Many educators wanted the grants to go directly to the institutions. Nonetheless the government left the money in the hands of the students, who could go wherever they chose. This subsidy therefore supported decentralized competitive finance.[60]

The American tax system allows deductions for tuition and educational materials, if essential to an individual's job. Nonprofit universities are tax-exempt, and their charitable benefactors can deduct donations to universities from their taxes. These various tax deductions are estimated to be worth at least $11 billion to universities each year.[61]

Historically universities and colleges benefited greatly from the Land Grant Acts of 1862 and 1890. The federal government gave free land to universities with few restrictions. The area of this land was equal to the size of Switzerland, and helped schools such as Cornell, MIT, Yale, and Texas A&M, among others.[62]

The G.I. Bill, passed in 1944, helped drive the expansion of American higher education in the postwar era. The bill sent 2.25 million veterans to school until its expiration in 1956, and helped create the expectation that any upwardly mobile person would pursue higher education. To its credit, the bill stipulated that the federal government could not exercise control over the funded institutions; in many cases the federal government did not even require accreditation. The bill thus funded higher education, but without weakening competitive constraints.[63]

Subsidies often corrode efficiency and flexibility, but American higher education has remained vital. Public universities compete on roughly the same terms as do private universities, and function in roughly the same manner. Public universities must compete for endowment dollars and for tuition revenue. American colleges and universities, whether private or public, receive funds from broadly similar sources. They look to national, state, and local governments, as well as business firms, alumni, foundations, private donors, churches, attached hospitals, and students (whose funds arrive in the form of tuition and fees).

Governance institutions have supported this flexibility, as each school enjoys autonomous governance in a broader, decentralized environment. In both state and private institutions, a unitary president is accountable to an independent board of trustees. Provosts and deans are appointed by the president and can be fired at his or her discretion. The presence of independent boards insulates the university from political pressure and allows unpopular decisions to be made. These boards make the American college and university system the most competitive in the world, as they typically preserve autonomy for even the public-sector institutions. The Continental model, in contrast, treats the university as a civil-service institution, subject to overarching control by a central bureaucratic authority. A ministry of education, or some comparable bureaucracy, controls university policy. Administrators tend to be elected within the institution, rather than appointed by a board of outsiders. Professors are formally civil servants, rather than independent agents.[64]

The autonomy of American universities has brought a corresponding flexibility. Many of the first American universities were set up as religious institutions, devoted to Protestant instruction. As late as the 1890s, for instance, most state universities still required their students to attend chapel services; some required Sunday church attendance as well. The University of Michigan, among many others, was an explicitly Christian institution, and state-sponsored chapel services became unusual only in the 1940s.[65] George Marsden (1994, p. 239) notes that "the University of Chicago arose out of the concern of Baptists that they were falling behind in the educational race in the West." In this century, the university has been one of the most important educational institutions in the history of the West. The early work on atomic physics was done at Chicago, and the Chicago school of economics has contributed greatly to market-oriented reforms around the world. Some critics (e.g., Holcombe 2000) complain that American nonprofit institutions have deviated from their original charters over time. These charges, however, often neglect the many beneficial changes in mission that have occurred.

In addition to its artistic achievements, American higher education, including public universities, is the envy of the world. Public-sector involvement has been greatest since the American system reached its peak. This does not demonstrate that state subsidy deserves the credit for the quality of the American system, but it does suggest that those subsidies have not destroyed quality. Most of the best universities in the world are located in the United States, and this designation includes many state universities, such as the University of Virginia, the University of Michigan, and the University of California at Berkeley. The system has produced numerous Nobel Prizes and has helped American-based scientists to dominate scientific communities around the world. The American university also has been a critical partner in high-technology enterprises and in biotechnology. Silicon Valley was built around the intellectual capital of Stanford and UC Berkeley. One study estimates that MIT graduates and faculty have founded at least four thousand companies, which would rank twenty-fourth in the world if they were considered an independent nation. University hospitals, such as those at Johns Hopkins, Harvard, and UC San Francisco, are noteworthy as well.[66]

## Overly Academic Culture?

Critics charge that university-supported culture is excessively abstract, refined, "bloodless," and out of touch with the American people. The painter Harold Altman, who himself taught at Pennsylvania State University, remarked: "in most departments throughout the country, perhaps less than a fraction of 1 percent [of the arts faculty] are worth a damn. . . . And that applies to . . . all the faculties . . . that I've seen. There are few university artists of superior quality. There are lots of people who are dead as artists."[67] He noted: "so many times I say to myself, 'What the [expletive deleted] am I doing in this university? What am I doing with these people here? Am I crazy?"[68]

Critics sometimes contrast contemporary university life with the lives of the great nineteenth- or early-twentieth-century writers. Herman Melville worked on a whaling ship, and Joseph Conrad traveled extensively in the wilds of Southeast Asia. Jack London had a tumultuous career as a sailor before becoming a writer. Earlier, Cervantes fought in the Battle of Lepanto and spent time in prison. Today's university professor, in contrast, is portrayed as having spent his or her life with bookshelves and term papers. The modern university is considered a home for bloodless, self-referential writing.

This contrast, however, is overstated. Many notable writers of earlier times had relatively quiet or sedentary lives. Shakespeare appears to have had a normal life as an Elizabethan playwright, without much travel or explicit adventure. Edmund Spenser spent much of his life at court. At the extreme, to name one among many examples, Marcel

Proust was a sickly child, did not travel beyond Italy, and ended up spending much of his life in a cork-lined room. All these writers were full of passion, despite having had quiet lives on the surface. To the extent that the human condition is universal, we should expect to find writers hailing from a wide variety of backgrounds, which is indeed the case, both today and in earlier times.

Many university-based creators have spent significant parts of their lives in active and worldly endeavors. Jorge Bolet, the renowned romantic pianist, came from Cuba but spent the latter part of his life teaching at Indiana University. Janos Starker also ended up teaching at Indiana University, after pursuing an active public life in Hungary. The university system is often a refuge for individuals, frequently foreigners, who have had more than enough turmoil.

Jacob Lawrence, one of the leading African-American painters of this century, spent his early life in a foster home, and living in Harlem during the Harlem Renaissance. He also taught at several colleges and universities, starting with Black Mountain College in 1946, which was renowned for supporting artists. For sixteen years (1970–1986) he was a tenured full professor at the University of Washington, during which time he continued to paint.[69]

The American system continually imports nonacademic creative sources into academia, thus getting the best of both worlds. Universities, in effect, allow America to bid for creators from dangerous and uncomfortable places. The university gives creators a place to work, but it does not academize the entire world, and it can import talent from nonacademic environments.

University employment does make many American culture producers more academic than would be ideal. But at the same time the system provides career insurance for creators who pursue risky and adventurous lives. Individuals can invest in developing life experience with fewer worries about their long-run prospects for financial support, than would otherwise be the case. If an individual sets out to be a composer, he or she forgoes opportunities to acquire other talents or other forms of career certification. Tying to make it as a professional composer is a very risky venture. But if failed composers, or moderately successful composers, have the option of university jobs as fallbacks, more people will try in the first place. Philip Glass did not end up teaching in a university, but nonetheless universities provided implicit insurance for his risk taking.

The university also injects diversity into the broader societal discovery process. Faculty tenure is based on two principles: free inquiry and intellectual autonomy. Taken together, these principles also could be described by the less-favorable-sounding phrase "lack of accountability." A tenured faculty member simply is not very accountable to deans and department chairs. This absence of accountability, while it comes under heavy criticism, is part of the virtue of the university. The university works by generating and evaluating ideas according to novel and independent principles, relative to the rest of society. Direct commercial considerations drive most sources of ideas in society, including corporate research and development, commercial culture, advertising, and celebrity culture. The university is an alternative and complementary mechanism for producing and evaluating social ideas. In the university professors are, at least in theory, insulated from direct commercial pressures. Most academic rewards are determined by peer evaluation.

Tenure and nonaccountability work especially well for a process that depends on intellectual or creative superstars. The average producer might use lack of accountability to shirk, or to pursue self-indulgent ideas of little value. But the superstars will use lack of accountability to pursue their own visions without outside hindrance. We like to think of "creative freedom" as good and "lack of accountability" as bad, but in fact they are two sides of the same coin. If most of the value added comes from the superstars, the gains from their freedom may exceed the losses from the shirking of the average producer. Given that most artistic experiments are failures, effective discovery procedures often succeed by supporting the extremes, rather than trying to generate a good outcome in every attempt.

Since we should evaluate institutions as a bundle, the excesses of the university, which include conservatism and overspecialization, should be seen as part of a broader picture. All methods of producing ideas involve biases. The question is whether these biases tend to offset or exaggerate the other biases—usually commercial—that are already present in the broader system. To the extent the biases are offsetting, the benefits of the university are robust. Counterintuitively, one of the great virtues of commercial society is its ability to augment noncommercial sources of support, including the university. Academic institutions, whatever their particular failings, increase the diversity of the social discovery process, including discovery in the creative arts.

# 3. Direct Subsidies:
## Are They Too Conservative?

Direct subsidies to the arts have two potential major rationales. First, the NEA and other governmental institutions might act as venture capitalists to stimulate new artistic ideas. They would seek out new and untried artists, with the hope of picking winners. The Work Projects Administration (WPA) of Roosevelt's New Deal served this function. Such policies may be based on the idea that the market does a poor job in evaluating new artists, or on the simple belief that more new art is a good thing. Policies of this kind would respond to the decentralization argument, namely the need to provide more varied sources of support for the arts.

Alternatively, direct subsidies might target works of high culture that have stood a test of time. We might use government policy to promote access to the works of Herman Melville, Emily Dickinson, and Winslow Homer, or perhaps to promote European high culture. Aesthetic arguments—make society more artistic in orientation, even at the expense of efficiency—might justify such policies, although economic arguments typically would not. This kind of intervention can cite the prestige argument for a possible justification.

American direct subsidies, and the NEA in particular, are currently split between a venture capitalist role and preserving the best of the past. They try to do a bit of both and to be all things to all people, if only to ensure their political survival. The resulting policies and institutions have lost their role as major drivers of excellence. In this chapter we will see how direct subsidies have developed through American history, what ends direct subsidies have achieved, and where they have failed.

Unlike many arts advocates, I do not regard the case for direct subsidies as self-evident. Governments may make matters worse rather than better. Duke Ellington, painters Edward Hopper and Thomas Hart Benton, poet W. H. Auden, and writers George Jean Nathan, Gilbert Seldes, and John Cheever all opposed government arts programs. Symphony orchestras applied for NEA funds only in 1970; the delay was due to their suspicion of the idea. An earlier (1953) poll of the American Symphony Orchestra League had found that 91 percent of the governing boards of the orchestras strongly opposed federal art subsidies of any kind. Painter John Sloan noted: "Sure, it would be fine to have a Ministry of the Fine Arts in this country. Then we'd know where the enemy is." Another painter, Larry Rivers, claimed that "the government taking a role in art is like a gorilla threading a needle. It is at first cute, then clumsy, and most of all impossible."[1]

The idea of direct subsidies "sounds good" to many art lovers, but such subsidies do not always encourage artistic creativity. Some direct subsidies discourage artistic output. European orchestras are far more heavily subsidized than their American counterparts, but they offer many fewer performances in a year. Given their higher base income, the European orchestras do not need to play and tour as much to stay in business. Other times the subsidy displaces private output with public output. If the government hires a successful artist to create a public sculpture, the result may be more government-funded sculptures but fewer privately funded sculptures.

Let us now turn to the history and nature of American direct funding, with an eye toward which of these programs have proven most successful.


## The Evolution of Direct Funding


American arts policy has been haphazard and scattered from the beginning. The first significant direct subsidy to the American arts came in

1817, when John Trumbull was commissioned to paint four pictures, commemorating the Revolutionary War, to be hung in the Capitol. Both the expenditure ($32,000) and the quality of the pictures were controversial, discouraging subsequent government arts patronage. In 1832 Congress commissioned Horace's Greenough's sculpture of George Washington. The sculpture arrived in 1841 but was removed from the Capitol grounds because many viewers thought it not dignified enough. The nineteenth century brought a variety of other commissions for government buildings, most notably works of Constantino Brumidi and Albert Bierstadt, but no formal arts policy was in place.[2]

This patchwork approach continued. In 1846 Congress created the Smithsonian Institution, from a bequest of materials from explorer James Smithson. The early Smithsonian, however, had more to do with science than with the arts. In 1859 President James Buchanan appointed a National Art Commission, but it was disbanded two years later. The Department of the Interior supported attempts to record and catalog the Indian arts, usually within the context of geographic and surveying work. The government did not care about Indian arts at the time, but many of the commissioned surveyors had a keen interest in Indian culture and ethnography. The Tarnsey Act of 1893 allowed Congress to use private architects for federal buildings, rather than the Treasury architects; this improved architectural quality in many cases. In 1910 Congress established the National Commission of Fine Arts, which supervised design and decoration for federal buildings but did not otherwise engage in cultural policy. The commission still meets one day a month to oversee the development of Washington, D.C., and to plan federal buildings. President Theodore Roosevelt improved the nation's coinage, which he valued as a means of artistic communication and a symbol of national strength. He befriended and commissioned artists toward this end, and directed the national mint to make sure these designs were executed.[3]

In this largely private environment American culture flourished. Herman Melville, Emily Dickinson, Mark Twain, Winslow Homer, and Henry James, among others, did their best work in the mid- to late nineteenth century. Early forms of the blues, country music, and jazz germinated. Performances of Shakespeare were widespread. Many of the American Indian arts hit peaks. The early twentieth century saw this boom continue. Jazz, blues, and country music came to full fruition, and spread through radio and recordings. Hollywood became a moviemaking power. Thomas Eakins and John Singer Sargent were leading American painters. Modernist art and literature came to America, as evidenced by F. Scott Fitzgerald, William Faulkner, Marsden Hartley, Arthur Dove, and many others. The skyscraper put America in the forefront of modern architecture, while Beaux Arts, Art Nouveau, and Art Deco styles flourished on smaller scales. The Craftsman Bungalow, the Arts and Crafts house, the Pueblo Revival, and the Prairie Style all flourished around the turn of the century. For the first time, American culture became a world leader, most of all in movies, music, and architecture. Government played little or no role in these developments.

## A New Deal

The New Deal gave the U.S. government direct responsibility for funding artworks on a large scale, most of all through the Works Progress Administration (WPA, later called the Work Projects Administration). The WPA, which was initiated in 1935, continued two earlier New Deal programs, the Federal Emergency Relief Administration (FERA) and the Public Works of Art Project (PWAP, organized through the Treasury Department to decorate public buildings and parks with art). At their peak New Deal policies provided the largest public arts programs in the world. They employed forty thousand artists (five thousand per year at the peak), commissioned 1,371 public murals, supported a Federal Theatre Project, a Federal Writers' Project, and a Federal Music Project. Total expenditures for all WPA arts programs, over the course of the New Deal, ran in the neighborhood of $160 million, which would equal slightly more than $2 billion in 2005 dollars.[4]

Of all the government arts programs in American history, the WPA was arguably the most successful. The WPA operated in fertile conditions. America had entered an era of remarkable creativity, and first-rate artists were plentiful in many genres. Many of these artists had a difficult time making ends meet, in part because of the Depression, and they were eager to participate in government programs. The more poorly markets are working, for whatever reason, the greater the chance that government arts programs will boost the quantity and quality of creative enterprise.

Like so many government programs for the arts, the WPA was driven by nonartistic motives. The WPA was first and foremost an antipoverty program, and most of the expenditures had nothing to do with the arts at all. Most WPA funds recipients had to be taken off the relief rolls; this ensured that most of the recipients were needy artists, rather than wealthy and established creators. Often artists were expected to prove their poverty. Many artists were ineligible because they were self-employed, or had been unemployed *before* the Depression arrived, or were successfully employed. The WPA therefore targeted a specific cross section of artists, namely previously employed individuals who had recently fallen on hard times. The individuals in this cross section had some chance of having talent, yet they were poor enough that government support made a difference. In fact over 60 percent of WPA artists received at least three-quarters of their income from the program; fewer than 10 percent received less than a quarter of their income from the program. According to one estimate, the average recipient in 1935 was only thirty-two years of age. Given this constituency, the WPA was able to make a real difference.[5]

Once the artist could show financial need, the WPA distributed funds on relatively indiscriminate principles. In the visual arts, anyone who could produce a framed canvas qualified as an "artist" and could apply for support; most of the recipients were not artists as we would understand the term. When the WPA ended during the war, government warehouses had to auction off thousands of canvases by the pound. Other pictures were burnt, taken home by bureaucrats, or, in one case, sold to a plumber for use as pipe insulation.[6]

These anecdotes may sound catastrophic, but they reflect the decentralization that made the program work. The WPA, in addition to supporting numerous frauds, gave many different would-be creators a chance to prove themselves. The decision to enter the program was, to a considerable extent, up to the would-be artist, rather than the government. The number of great-painters-to-be at the time was high enough, and the WPA net was cast widely enough, that the institution supported many creators of significance. The WPA succeeded because it embodied decentralization, rather than because of effective peer review, or because its director had a first-rate artistic eye.

The WPA and related programs supported Jackson Pollock, Arshile Gorky, Philip Guston, Willem de Kooning, Mark Rothko, and Ad Reinhardt, who became top American artists after the Second World War. From the earlier crop, the Roosevelt programs funded Stuart Davis, Marsden Hartley, Ben Shahn, Joseph Stella, Grant Wood, Jacob Lawrence, Edward Hopper, Reginald Marsh, John Steuart Curry, John Sloan, Bradley Walker Tomlin, and Rockwell Kent. The Missouri murals of Thomas Hart Benton, arguably his most important works, were WPA projects as well. It would be hard to produce a more impressive list of American painters from this period.[7]

It is interesting to compare the WPA to the Treasury Section arts programs of the same era. The Treasury programs were commissioned by panels of art experts, whereas the WPA selection method was closer to an arbitrary free-for-all. Francis V. O'Connor (1971, p. 108) described the Treasury Section as "an excellent example of a government patron tightly controlling all aspects of the creative process in order to acquire the 'best' art at minimum financial and political risk to itself. While it occasionally got what it wanted, it did so by stifling the very mural movement it hoped to establish and maintain." His description of the WPA differs: "The WPA . . . , on the other hand . . . achieved those results which are the goals of any honest and enlightened patron — namely the nurturing of talent and innovation."

Sculptor Robert Cronbach worked for both programs and offered a comparable estimate of their merits. He greatly favored the WPA over the peer-reviewed Treasury programs. He noted that "the WPA program enabled a great number of artists to work continuously in their own field," and that "if one realizes that the most vital and important art of the last 150 years has been the work that was non-official and non-commissioned, one must admit that to give a large number of artists of many different persuasions an opportunity to work steadily is a most important achievement." He noted the "inherent limits" of the jury system, and claimed, "It cannot enable new art to develop, or a wide range of art and artists to flourish."[8]

The WPA was remarkably broad-minded in its artistic funding. The preservation and stimulation of the folk arts of New Mexico owed a considerable debt to WPA funds; in 1999 the Museum of International Folk Art in Santa Fe staged an entire exhibit of WPA-sponsored folk art from the American Southwest, mostly of very high quality.[9]

New Mexico sculptor Patrocino Barela, now considered one of the finest "Outsider" artists of the period, received his start with the New Deal art programs, first the FERA and then the WPA. Until he started working for the government, Barela was unable to earn a living as a carver. The WPA, however, enabled him to give up his odd jobs and his sheepherding. Shortly thereafter he was exhibiting his works, and in 1936 his sculptures at the Museum of Modern Art received rave reviews, causing *Time* magazine to call him "discovery of the year." When the New Deal arts programs were disbanded, Barela went back to herding sheep. Ironically the WPA held him back in part, since government officials tried to protect him from "unscrupulous" private art dealers and refused to forward gallery commissions to him.[10]

In the area of literature the Federal Writers, Project provided support to John Steinbeck, Robert Frost, Conrad Aiken, Richard Wright, Saul Bellow, Ralph Ellison, Kenneth Rexroth, Nelson Algren, Frank Yerby, and Willard Motley. As part of the Florida project, Zora Neale Hurston wrote three books in three years, including her now-famous *Their Eyes Were Watching God* (1937). The "Negro studies" movement had its origin in a number of WPA projects, including the collection of ex-slave narratives.[11]

Like the painting programs, the writers' program supported both geniuses and dregs. The WPA funded a large number of communists who used the support to write political propaganda. The New York office was renowned for the fistfights between Stalinists and Trotskyites. Even the best writers often found their talents wasted. Saul Bellow worked for the Writers' Project, but he found himself compiling lists of magazines held in a library. He reportedly envied the more "interesting" work of two of his colleagues, one of whom covered pigeon racing in Chicago, the other of whom wrote high school vocational textbooks.[12]

The New Deal programs covered virtually every aspect of the arts. The Music Project commissioned works by Aaron Copland and Virgil Thomson, awarded prizes to William Schumann and a young Elliott Carter, and helped sponsor new orchestras in Pittsburgh, Utah, and Buffalo. The Joint Committee on Folk Arts (not part of the Music Project) supported John and Alan Lomax in their effort to record American blues and folk songs; these recordings continue to sell today and are considered essential musical documents of the era.[13]

The Federal Theatre Project sponsored Orson Welles, who among other things directed an all-black version of Macbeth, set in Haiti. T. S. Eliot's *Murder in the Cathedral* was staged. John Houseman, Lee J. Cobb, and Elia Kazan worked for the project as well. Arthur Miller and Clifford Odets began their careers writing plays for the government. In total fourteen thousand actors were employed to play to about twenty-five million spectators.[14]

Funding for the New Deal photography programs came from the Department of Agriculture and the Civilian Conservation Corps in addition to the WPA. These subsidies helped make the 1930s a golden age of documentary photography, supporting such notable photographers as Dorothea Lange, Walker Evans, Russell Lee, Ben Shahn, John Vachon, Marion Post Wolcott, and Arthur Rothstein. As with so many of the New Deal programs, the motive was often nonartistic. The USDA photography program, in particular, produced propaganda for New Deal programs. They encouraged photographers to depict federal bureaucrats as sympathetic friends of the farmers, and as concerned with helping ordinary Americans make a good living. According to one account, "The government always appeared as friendly advisor, and the changes it introduced were best."[15]

The WPA was never intended to serve as a permanent program. Most WPA activity wound down when America entered the Second World War, and the program was halted entirely in 1943. In 1938, legislation was proposed to create a permanent Bureau of Fine Arts. The bill was debated extensively but failed to receive sufficient support. America thus turned its back on the idea of government-supported art though, as we will see, not on the practice.[16]

The WPA relied on unique conditions, and its success has not proven to be replicable. Swiss arts support in the 1930s resembled WPA programs in significant regards, yet did not enlist a comparably talented set of top creators. In more recent times the Dutch government has offered fairly indiscriminate support to its painters, often targeting the young, yet without producing notable successes. Those programs have not identified or produced the next Mondrian or Rembrandt. The Dutch government has accumulated a large number of subsidized paintings in warehouses, and current debate revolves around how to get rid of the works.[17]

In the 1970s the United States experimented with the use of CETA (Comprehensive Employment and Training Act) funds to create public-service jobs for artists. In 1976, this program employed ten thousand artists and related workers, at a cost of approximately $60 million for that year.[18] A formal "Artists-in-Residence" program ran from 1977 to 1981, employing between ten thousand and twenty thousand artists a year at its peak.[19] Yet this episode brought few notable artistic successes and showed no signs of having replicated the peaks of the WPA. The roster of unemployed creators in the 1970s was not as impressive as it had been forty years earlier. The world now is wealthier, the Great Depression is long over, and artistic institutions do a better job of spotting talent early.

## Art and Foreign Policy Propaganda Programs

Contrary to common opinion, the passing of the WPA did not end direct subsidies to the arts. In fact, direct governmental funding of the arts peaked in the Cold War era. The WPA did not lead to a permanent arts agency, but government extended its hand in the arts through foreign policy. Policymakers saw the arts as a primary weapon in the Cold War against the Soviet Union and a means of spreading the American way. Once again, arts programs were driven by nonartistic motives.

Cultural imperialism has driven governmental support, and destruction, of the arts throughout history. The Roman and Chinese empires viewed acculturation as a means of spreading their rule, and encouraged the arts toward this end. The European colonial powers, especially France, sought to carry their cultures to their colonies. The settlement of the American West and Midwest, and the corresponding treatment of the native Indians, was a form of cultural policy, often enforced by violence.

The most drastic example of cultural policy came in the occupied countries immediately after the Second World War. The United States government instituted comprehensive cultural control in Germany, Austria, and Japan. In Austria and Germany, the U.S. Information Services Branch controlled the presentation of virtually all cultural activities, including films, theater, concerts, radio, newspapers, magazines and books, advertisements, circuses, balls, and carnival festivities. The American occupiers saw cultural control as essential to denazification and the reconstruction of a healthy society. Broadcasting sovereignty was not returned to West Germany until 1955. In Japan censorship and control covered every form of media and entertainment, at one point suppressing Tolstoy's *War and Peace*, as well as any Japanese cultural product that might appear militaristic.[20]

As Germany and Japan showed their willingness to follow the American lead, American cultural programs evolved from control to the export of propaganda. As the Cold War developed, politicians supported the performance of American arts abroad to counter Soviet propaganda about the vitality of communism. They believed that if American culture could be shown to be strong and creative, democracy would look good.

The Republican administration of Eisenhower spent more on cultural outreach programs, in real terms, than was later spent on the NEA. These programs were spread out over several agencies (see below), but the best available estimate of their scope is as seen in table 1.[21] For purposes of contrast, note that NEA expenditures hit a maximum of just over $175 million in 1992. If we convert the 1953 expenditure on foreign cultural programs to 1992 dollars, the sum is roughly $690 million.

These cultural programs were part of a much larger machinery of foreign propaganda programs. At its peak, the United States foreign propa-

TABLE 1
U.S. Cultural Outreach Spending

| Year | Budget (Millions) |
| --- | --- |
| 1947 | $19 |
| 1948 | 14 |
| 1949 | 27 |
| 1950 | 37 |
| 1951 | 56 |
| 1952 | 115 |
| 1953 | 129 |
| 1954 | 90 |
| 1955 | 100 |
| 1956 | 110 |

ganda machine spent $2 billion a year, employed a staff of more than ten thousand, and reached 150 countries. These operations were larger than the twenty biggest United States public relations firms combined.[22]

Twentieth-century cultural outreach programs had their roots in the late 1930s, when the United States attempted to publicize the "American way of life" in Latin America. This model was extended after the Second World War. The Smith-Mundt Act of 1948, in particular, institutionalized the use of culture as Cold War propaganda. This act called for the spread of information abroad about the government and culture of the United States, thereby creating the Office of International Information and Educational Exchange (OIE) and the United States Information Service (USIS). The Voice of America (VOA), expanded in the late 1940s, transmitted radio programs, often of a cultural nature, as did Radio Free Europe and Radio Liberty. In 1953 the United States Information Agency (USIA) was created to spread a favorable American image around the world.[23]

The logic of bureaucracy suggests why these programs relied so heavily on culture. Few foreign audiences are keen to hear American political propaganda. But the propaganda agencies needed to keep audiences to justify their existence. Toward this end they turned to culture, and typically they sought to promote entertaining culture, if only to keep their audiences and thus their budgets. Through pure accident, this was the most customer-driven American arts program in history.

State Department and USIA programs sent leading American orchestras, singers, jazz musicians, musical shows, and instrumentalists on tours of the world, at U.S. government expense. The United States government ran its own 120-piece symphony orchestra and a swing dance band, both said to be among the best of their kind in Europe.[24]

The later domestic arts programs, such as the NEA, pale in comparison. Over nineteen years (1948–1967) the Marshall Plan had a Media Guarantee Program that distributed 134 million copies of American books to Europe. In 1970 the United States Information Agency was publishing 140 magazines with a total circulation of approximately 30 million; during the 1980s the USIA operated 135 libraries in eighty-three countries (interest in that agency peaked under the Reagan administration). A 1969 estimate noted that 25 million people visited these libraries annually.[25]

By 1980 there were 101 government-sponsored radio stations, often directed toward the Iron Curtain. In one year, 1983, Voice of America alone received $1.3 billion in government funds for modernization. In the 1980s the station was estimated to reach 80 million listeners a day, excluding China. The propaganda broadcast by these stations usually included culture; the USIA has claimed that half of VOA broadcasts are devoted to culture and education, rather than to politics in the narrower sense.[26]

Jazz promotion, through VOA and other government-sponsored radio stations, has been one of the most successful American arts programs. Willis Conover emceed the VOA *Music USA* program for twenty-five years and was the single most influential ambassador for American jazz in Eastern Europe. A Cold War survey indicated that Conover was the best-known living American in Poland. American jazz spread as far as the Soviet gulags, where prisoners started their own bands. These jazz programs can be thought of as a form of artistic famine relief.[27]

The State Department favored jazz as well. The art form is uniquely American in origin, relatively inexpensive to send on tour, and has proved greatly popular with foreign audiences. Furthermore jazz concerts ostensibly showed that not all African-Americans were oppressed or cowering in ghettos, as Communist propaganda of the time was alleging. The State Department funded tours by Leontyne Price, Dizzy Gillespie, Marian Anderson, and the Martha Graham Dance Troupe. Gershwin's opera *Porgy and Bess,* with a primarily black cast, toured for over a decade with government support and received an enthusiastic reception around the world.[28]

The United States, of course, received Soviet culture in exchange. Americans were able to see the Moiseyev Folk Dance Ensemble, the Bolshoi Ballet, and the Kirov Ballet, in addition to numerous classical pianists and violinists.[29]

Cultural outreach programs continue today, but their scope has declined. Even before the end of the Cold War, the budget of the USIA and the cultural activities of the CIA had been pared back. The fall of the Soviet Union only continued this trend. The USIA, however, still runs "artistic ambassador" programs that support performances by U.S. artists abroad. The Arts America budget, for instance, has run in the neighborhood of $3.4 million annually for the last five years. Cultural broadcasts continue through the Voice of America, Radio and Television Marti (aimed toward Cuba), and World Net, although these programs have lost much of their importance.[30]

Cultural outreach programs appear to be coming back into fashion, out of desire to project a more positive U.S. image to Islamic cultures and the Middle East. The recently established Radio Sawa received a $35 million grant from Congress to broadcast popular Arabic music, and news from an American perspective, in the Middle East. The station has reached number one among listeners under thirty in Amman, and is very popular in Baghdad and Kuwait. It is estimated that the station reaches 86 percent of the target audience (seventeen- to twenty-eight-year-olds) each week. If anything, the station has been criticized for concentrating too much on music rather than too little.[31]

Congress also has allocated $62 million for an Arabic-language TV station, Al Hurra (Free One), to broadcast throughout the region. In addition to news and documentaries, the station offers movies, music, and cultural commentary.[32]

The presentation of foreign music has precedents in Voice of America history. VOA has presented Indian classical music, Haitian creole music, and folk musics from around the world, in each case to the native country of origin. The Laotian style of *mohlam* was originally presented by troubadours wandering from village to village. The Communists banned this style of music for some time, and VOA played a significant role in its revival.[33]

Outreach programs, in addition to distributing culture abroad, also boosted culture at home. Jazz, modern dance, and avant-garde theater, in particular, benefited from federal patronage. The performers received financial support and a new air of high-cultural legitimacy, thereby widening their audience base. Jazz became a source of pride for many Americans. Albert Ailey's dance company used government-sponsored tours to stay in business. Government support allowed Dizzy Gillespie to assemble and maintain an expensive big band, which led to some of his most important music.[34]

The federal role was not restricted to the State Department, as the CIA funded the arts through the Congress for Cultural Freedom (CCF). The CCF funded a support network for liberal and left-wing intellectuals and creators who were opposed to communism and, as part of that program, funded a broad network of cultural activities. The CCF supported an extensive European tour of the Boston Symphony Orchestra, for instance, to show that America was culturally advanced.

Recipients of CCF funds included Saul Bellow, W. H. Auden, Jackson Pollock, Robert Motherwell, Lionel Trilling, Arthur Koestler, John Steinbeck, Upton Sinclair, Herbert Read, and Robert Penn Warren. The CCF supported the European premieres of works by such American composers as Samuel Barber, Leonard Bernstein, Elliott Carter, Aaron Copland, George Gershwin, Gian Carlo Menotti, and Virgil Thomson. The theater program supported works by Lillian Hellman, Eugene O'Neill, Thornton Wilder, Tennessee Williams, William Saroyan, and John Steinbeck. The CCF sponsored the literary/political/cultural magazine *Encounter* for many years and *Kenyon Review* and *Partisan Review* for a shorter time, among other publications.[35]

Given program secrecy, the extent of CIA involvement is difficult to gauge, especially since the money was usually laundered through private foundations. A 1976 congressional study of foundation grants in the mid-1960s found that of the 700 grants involving more than $10,000 (1963–1966, and not just for culture), at least 108 involved CIA funding. Half of the large grants for international activities during this same period involved CIA funding. *The New York Times* estimated that the CIA supported the publication of at least one thousand books, including such odd choices as translations of the poetry of T. S. Eliot. Frances Saunders (1999, pp. 1, 129) describes the effort in terms of "vast resources," and describes the CIA as America's "Ministry of Culture" during this period. Michael Josselson, head of the CCF, was a CIA agent during that time.[36]

In the visual arts the CIA played a loose role in promoting Abstract Expressionism. A few small CIA-based grants supported the exhibit of Abstract Expressionist paintings abroad. More significantly, CIA and corporate networks had close ties with the Museum of Modern Art in New York City, especially through Nelson Rockefeller, who served as chairman of the board of the museum. MOMA promoted the Abstract Expressionist movement once it got off the ground. Rockefeller called Abstract Expressionism "free-enterprise painting," largely because it did not have the left-wing political messages associated with muralist art. Whether the CIA played a direct role here, or whether CIA-affiliated individuals were simply acting in private capacities, is a moot point.[37]

The foreign-policy motivations of these cultural outreach programs led inevitably to censorship and selective presentation. For instance, the America House institution brought books and records to European audiences, but only on a selective basis. Sherwood Anderson, Leonard Bernstein, Pearl S. Buck, Aaron Copland, John Dewey, John Dos Passos, Theodore Dreiser, W.E.B. DuBois, Albert Einstein, George Gershwin, Dashiell Hammett, Norman Mailer, Arthur Miller, Reinhold Niebuhr, Arthur M. Schlesinger, Mickey Spillane, Virgil Thomson, and Frank Lloyd Wright, among others, were all censored from America House. (Note that some of the banned creators, such as Copland, had received support from earlier New Deal arts programs.) From European literature, Boccaccio, Flaubert, Stendahl, and Thomas Mann were kept out as well. Most ironically, Thomas Paine's *Common*

*Sense* and Thoreau's *Walden* were banned, despite (because of?) the status of those books as paeans to liberty. For a while, the USIA refused to fund the exhibition of any art produced after 1917, the year of the Russian Revolution.[38]

The CCF had to keep its nature hidden from public view. To promote an open society, the CCF sought to glorify the artistic products of democracy. Yet the support for promoting these products abroad came under the guise of secrecy. Thomas Braden, who supervised the cultural activities of the CIA, noted: "Back in the early 1950s . . . the idea that Congress would have approved many of our projects was about as likely as the John Birch Society's approving Medicare."[39]

Conservative critics attacked many of the Cold War–era cultural outreach programs, in a manner reminiscent to contemporary debates over the NEA. In the late 1940s, conservative critics charged that an exhibit of abstract art to Latin America promoted "pseudo-art." One representative was incensed after seeing a Martha Graham dance performance of *Phaedras*, with its themes of overt sexuality and incest. A tour of Toscanini's Symphony of the Air orchestra was canceled, out of fear that four orchestra members had procommunist sympathies. The State Department was worried when Duke Ellington was photographed with his white female companion, during a government-sponsored tour of Turkey. Only the Kennedy assassination, which followed immediately, prevented a public scandal from breaking out.[40]

Michigan representative George Dondero was the most persistent critic of State Department arts programs. He charged that modern art was an enemy of liberty. In his view, for instance, Wassily Kandinsky, who had been a friend of Trotsky, unleashed on the czarist government "the black knight of the isms." By this he meant cubism, futurism, dadaism, expressionism, constructionism, surrealism, and abstractionism. These movements brought "depravity, decadence, and destruction." In addition to targeting government arts programs, he objected to the Museum of Modern Art, the European artists who came to America during the war ("A horde of foreign art manglers"), and the Abstract Expressionists.[41]

Despite these pressures, the outreach programs typically supported a high quality of culture. In part the anticommunist rhetoric of these programs insulated them from attacks from the right. One pressure was paramount, namely the need to select American artists who would show their country in a favorable light. This discriminated against "communists" and controversial works of literature and theater. Most of all outreach subsidies boosted audience entertainment. At the same time, the programs were often innovative and aesthetically novel. The emphasis on jazz and modern dance proved effective. The promotion of African-American culture was later seen as pathbreaking.[42]

## Contemporary Direct Subsidies

The direct subsidies of any single American arts program have remained small, but the number of programs has multiplied. The "fiscal starvation" of the NEA has received considerable publicity, but broader decentralizing movements have been operating at the same time. Let us start with the NEA and then move to other subsidy programs.

In its first year the NEA received an appropriation of $8 million, and by 1974 this figure had grown to $74 million. The agency continued to grow rapidly through the early 1980s to the level of approximately $150 million per annum. Growth then came slower in the 1980s, with the budget peaking at $175 million in 1992. A drastic cut came in 1996, when the budget fell below $100 million for the first time since 1977. It has stayed in this range since, and circa 2005 it has crossed the $120 million threshold. Even at their peak, however, these expenditures have been minuscule relative to arts-related spending in the private sector. For purposes of comparison, the 1997 movie *Titanic* cost roughly $200 million to make. In 1983, revenue from Michael Jackson's *Thriller* album exceeded NEA expenditures for that year.[43]

The NEA is an independent government agency whose chairperson reports directly to the president. The chairperson, who must be confirmed by the Senate, is responsible for grant decisions. External panels of reviewers, appointed by the chairperson, assist agency staff members. A panel typically has between five and twenty members, who meet periodically to review grant applications. Most panel members are recognized experts in the relevant area, although each panel is expected to represent diverse viewpoints. The NEA was not originally based on peer review, but the large number of proposals forced the agency to move away from internal evaluation. While the chairperson is responsible for final decisions, he or she relies heavily on the panel recommendations.

NEA grants have varied in their degree of directness. The agency had the authority (since restricted) to give grants to individual artists. Alternatively, the agency can make grants to arts institutions. The infamous Robert Mapplethorpe exhibit was funded through a $30,000 grant to the Institute of Contemporary Art in Philadelphia, explicitly for that purpose. Support for Andres Serrano's *Piss Christ* was one step further removed. A general grant was given to the Southeastern Center of Contemporary Art (SECCA), in Winston-Salem, North Carolina. The NEA never made a direct decision to support Serrano or the show but rather gave SECCA the autonomy to distribute a $15,000 subgrant as it saw fit.[44]

Although the NEA receives most of the attention in public debate, in reality it is a small part of American arts policy. Governmental arts support comes from a wide range of public-sector institutions.

The Smithsonian Institution has expanded in scope since its origin in 1846 and now runs fifteen museums, maintains research centers, manages the National Zoo, and is affiliated with the National Gallery of Art. The institution attracts twenty-five million visitors a year, or forty million a year if traveling exhibits are counted. It has branches in New York; Cambridge, Massachusetts; Detroit; San Francisco; Annapolis; and several other parts of the United States, although the major museums are in the District of Columbia.[45]

The Smithsonian is an independent institution inside the federal government. The governing body is a board of regents, with some members drawn from the United States government. Much of the Smithsonian budget comes from Congress (in fiscal 2004 the net budget authority was $488 million); additional government contracts and grants can run up to nearly $100 million per year. The endowment has stood as high as $755 million. Unlike most other government arts programs, the Smithsonian receives significant private funds; in 2003 the Smithsonian raised over $200 million.[46]

Much of the growth of the Smithsonian, especially in the arts, came during the reign of S. Dillon Ripley as secretary, which started in 1964. He added the Hirshhorn Museum, the National Portrait Gallery, the National Collection of Fine Arts, the Renwick Gallery, and the Cooper-Hewitt Museum of Decorative Arts and Design to the institution. The Smithsonian also began administering the National Museum Act, which invests money to help improve museum professional standards.[47]

The National Gallery of Art, one of the premier art museums in America, received $79 million in 2003 from the federal government (this allocation is independent and not on Smithsonian ledgers). More generally, the American government showed an unusual degree of entrepreneurship in building this collection. The gallery was initiated in 1937 but inaugurated in 1941, outside the aforementioned New Deal arts programs. The Mellon family gave much of the art; it has been speculated that the gift was in return for the IRS stopping a tax fraud suit against Mellon. The Widener bequest, also central to the collection, came about when the federal government agreed to pay the Wideners' gift tax to the state of Pennsylvania. The museum also recruited the Kress, Chester Dale, and Rosenwald donations to the collection.[48]

The Corporation for Public Broadcasting (CPB) supports noncommercial radio and television programs. The CPB, founded in 1967, is a private nonprofit corporation, whose board is chosen by presidential appointment. The CPB provides funds to the Public Broadcasting Service (PBS), National Public Radio (NPR), and Public Radio International (PRI). Almost three-quarters of CPB funds are given directly to individual television and radio stations.

The 330 or so National Public Radio stations run programming on both popular and high culture. As for PBS, it is estimated that about 28 percent of the programs deal with culture. Three large PBS stations—Boston, New York, and Washington—produce more than half of the national programs, with the remainder being local products or imported from abroad. Other PBS shows have come from Great Britain, including *Masterpiece Theater, Monty Python's Flying Circus*, and *The Prisoner*.[49]

The CPB is explicitly directed to maintain "objectivity and balance" in the programs it funds. By law, the governing board of ten may not contain more than six members from any single political party. The CPB cannot itself schedule, advertise, or transmit programs, largely to alleviate fears of a "government television network." Despite these precautions, the Gingrich Republicans focused on the CPB as a major target of attack for its partisan programming, and it just narrowly escaped elimination. More recently the CPB has been perceived as taking a more centrist or conservative tone.[50]

The CPB appropriation for 2004 is $380 million. That being said, public television relies on many other sources of support. In a typical year the federal government supplies no more than 15 percent of the public television budget through grants and another few percent through direct contracts. State and local governments, often working with public universities, put up 30 percent or so. The remainder comes from viewer memberships, subscriptions, and corporate and foundation support. Over time public television has become more commercial in its orientation, in part because of competition from cable television. Critics charge that public broadcasting has become superfluous; about 86 percent of all American homes with television now have either a cable or satellite TV connection and thus have greater access to diversity and alternative programming.[51]

The Institute for Museum and Library Services (created in 1976, and formerly the Institute for Museum Services) spends $262 million a year (circa 2004) on museums, zoos, botanical gardens, and most of all libraries. The Arts and Artifacts Fund insures foreign objects lent to American museums and enables many art exhibitions. The Kennedy Center for the Performing Arts receives a direct congressional appropriation, currently in the neighborhood of $17 million; a few small programs also receive direct appropriations to support the arts in the District of Columbia.

The Art-in-Architecture (AiA) program is part of the General Services Administration (GSA). This program, originally modeled after the New Deal's Treasury Department Section of Painting and Sculpture, commissions and funds art for public buildings. The program started from a GSA decision in 1963. Since 1979 there has been a mandate that 0.5 percent of construction costs for federal buildings is to be spent on artwork. There is little systematic data on the program, but in calendar year 2001 it started projects with a collective budget of $4.5 million. As of 2001 the program had 260 projects and another 65 in the works. The most controversial artwork has been Richard Serra's *Tilted Arc* sculpture, which was removed from 26 Federal Plaza in New York City after employee complaints.[52]

Since the early 1970s AiA has relied on NEA panels to select artists for the commissions, although local communities add members to each panel. The final decision lies with the GSA administrator. To ensure diversity and dispel charges of favoritism, no more than a single work is commissioned from a particular artist, no matter how famous that artist may be. The program is not subject to direct congressional oversight, but past decisions have been aesthetically controversial, usually when AiA commissions sculpture with a contemporary style. From 1966 to 1973 the program was suspended in response to complaints, most of all concerning a Robert Motherwell mural in Boston.[53]

The National Trust for Historic Preservation dates from 1949, when it was chartered by Congress to preserve historic sites and receive donations toward that end. By the early 1990s, the trust received $7 million a year from the federal government, out of an annual budget in the range of $35 million. After the Republicans won Congress in 1996, however, the trust had to negotiate a phaseout of federal support. It has adjusted by increasing corporate licensing, offering more study tours, and increasing private fund-raising. The programs of the trust include preservation, management of historic sites, low-interest loans for preservation efforts, help with obtaining tax credits for preservation, and a legal defense fund for preservation efforts.[54]

The National Endowment for the Humanities (NEH), along with the Library of Congress, has programs to preserve old books by protecting the paper from deterioration. It also funds literary and artistic programs for public television, makes grants to museums for exhibits, and subsidizes low-price editions of American literary classics. Most NEH programs concern "the humanities" rather than "the arts," but the two concepts overlap in literature and some of the visual arts.[55]

Some of the most significant subsidies come through government agencies that are not usually associated with the arts. The U.S. Department of the Interior funds the arts and crafts of Native Americans and supports historic preservation efforts. Indian arts programs started in 1900, when the federal government supported efforts to train Indians in beadwork, basketry, and pottery. The Hoover administration provided subsidies to publicize Indian arts and crafts. The New Deal led to the creation of an Indian Arts and Crafts Board in the Interior Department. The board helped train Indian artists, organized promotional exhibits, organized producer cooperatives, helped publish a volume on the Indian arts, and set a governmental stamp of approval on "true" Indian arts and crafts, to distinguish the genuine products from the knockoffs. The board was small, however, with initial budgets in the range of $45,000 yearly.[56]

Despite the small size of the programs, the American government played an unprecedented direct role in the Indian art world. The board hired field representatives who lived with the Indians, coordinated their production activities, and gave them active advice on technique and design, as well as product marketing. Today the federal government maintains an active role in certifying products as genuinely "Indian," helping with marketing, and providing a consumer directory of Indian craftsworkers. The board runs three local museums of Indian art as well: the Sioux Indian Museum, the Museum of the Plains Indian, and the Southern Plains Indian Museum.[57]

The U.S. Forest Service funds demonstrations of folk arts and crafts, or performing arts activities more generally, in national forests. Many national parks have residency programs for artists, under the aegis of the Department of the Interior. A number of large-scale "earthworks" sculptures, such as those of Christo or Robert Smithson, have been created or placed on public lands.

Some of the largest government arts programs are run by the military. The United States Armed Services puts on regular cultural programs for military personnel and their families stationed abroad. This includes libraries, movie showings, and a large U.S. Army theater program. In essence, the government plans the cultural life for the 1.4 million individuals in the American armed forces (and their families), especially those stationed abroad.

The Army Art Collection, an extensive (ten thousand plus) holding of paintings, drawings, sketches, and watercolors, records the history of America at war. The army's official interest in art started in the First World War, when eight artists were commissioned to record American participation. A larger War Art Unit was established in 1942, which commissioned forty-two artists; later on in the war a joint effort was organized between *Life* magazine, Abbott Laboratories (a medical supply company), and the U.S. military. In the Vietnam War forty-two soldier artists, plus ten civilian artists, were commissioned to record the fighting. Since that time the commissioning of soldier and civilian artists has been common, even in peacetime. The army has no permanent art museum, but many of these artworks are on display at various army bases, installations, museums, and the Pentagon, and sometimes go on tour. The navy has an art museum, based at the U.S. Naval Academy at Annapolis. The military art held by the government includes works by such notable artists as Jacob Lawrence, Reginald Marsh, Horace Pippin, and Thomas Hart Benton.[58]

The USO (United Service Organizations Inc.) entertains soldiers by bringing in movie stars, musicians, and other celebrities. During World War II the USO employed 5,424 salaried entertainers and had a total show attendance of 172 million. The USO is not formally part of the federal government, but it is chartered by Congress and endorsed by the president, who is typically the honorary chairman. The USO today is smaller than during previous wars, but it still has 120 centers around the world and serves an average of 5 million individuals each year.[59]

The Department of Defense budget contains an allocation for military bands; this sum is now infamous for exceeding the entire NEA appropriation. On at least one occasion these bands supported art in the conventional sense; John Philip Sousa was conductor of the Marine Corps band from 1882 to 1890 and drew his later private band members from this time. The military band appropriation dates back to 1790; a 1995 estimate cites eighty-five military bands in total, with an aggregate budget usually in the neighborhood of $200 million.[60]

## State and Local Bodies

Subsidies from state governments have been growing in importance, relative to the NEA, since the 1960s. When the NEA started in 1965, few states had official arts councils or any kind of official arts policy. But from the beginning, the NEA gave at least 20 percent of its program funds to state and regional arts agencies, often in the form of block grants. The grants caused states to set up arts programs and councils to handle these grants; it is no coincidence that most state arts agencies were founded shortly after 1965. These institutions then expanded as they learned how to lobby their own state legislatures for funds. Most of the growth in the state institutions came in the 1980s. In 1979 NEA funds were 80 percent greater than state legislative appropriations; by 1989 the state appropriations were 60 percent higher. Most government growth in the United States, over the last twenty-five years, has come at the state and local level, and arts policy reflects this fact.[61]

The New York State Council on the Arts (NYSCA) alone has approached the size of the NEA in real terms. Its 2003 budget is $51.4 million, compared to the NEA's $122.5 million. But 40 percent of the latter is sent out to the states, leaving a real NEA budget of about $73.5 million.

In 2003 state-level arts expenditures were $354.5 million, but the amount fell to $273.7 million in 2004. Many state arts budgets came under strong fiscal pressures in part because state governments were required to balance their budgets with falling revenue. California cut its arts budget from $20 million to $2 million, Florida cut from $30 million to $6.7 million (which meant no grants at all for 2004), and Michigan cut from $22.5 to $11.8 million. Numerous other states enacted smaller cuts, and some states talked about phasing out their arts councils altogether. That being said, state arts funding now appears to be making a comeback or at least holding its ground.[62]

State arts councils have been compelled to change their rhetoric; they now cite economic arguments to an unprecedented extent. The councils have sought an image as net revenue attractors rather than revenue drains. The councils also take greater care to give politicians credit for the benefits they deliver, such as allowing politicians to pass out grant checks to recipient institutions at public ceremonies.

Utah, acting in 1899, was the first state to set up an arts agency. In Minnesota the State Art Society was founded in 1900 and spent its annual $7,000 appropriation on the organization of art exhibits. New York State had arts relief programs during the Great Depression, starting as early as 1932. The largest state agency, the New York State Council on the Arts, was founded in 1960 and provided a model for the NEA in terms of its funding patterns and system of peer review.[63]

State-level arts support does differ from NEA spending patterns in some regards. State programs tend to support smaller and more local organizations, and younger, less established artists. State programs also tend to be more accountable to politicians, and less influenced by arts professionals. State programs will more likely support arts "applications" in the fields of health, penology, and gerontology. Historically the NEA has had a greater emphasis on film (in part owing to grants to the American Film Institute), literature, and design arts but less on music, theater, and the visual arts, relative to state spending. State arts budgets exhibit more year-to-year volatility than does the NEA, largely because of the volatility of local state economies.[64]

In many cases cultural nonprofits receive a direct line-item appropriation from the state. In Connecticut, line-item appropriations have accounted for as much as 73.7 percent of total state arts spending. A few states (Alabama, California, Illinois, Missouri, Montana, Rhode Island, and West Virginia) hover in the 30 to 50 percent range, but line-item appropriations are small for the median case and often are zero. On average line-item spending accounts for 16 percent of state arts expenditures.[65]

There is no complete estimate of total arts expenditures at the local level. Nonetheless the U.S. Urban Arts Federation conducts periodic polls of its members. It forecast 2003 expenditures of $338 million at the local urban level. The single largest spender is the New York City Department of Cultural Affairs, which in 2004 spent $118.8 million; the San Francisco Arts Commission was next at $25.5 million.[66]

Local and urban subsidies have a scattered history. After the success of the Chicago World's Fair in 1893, many American cities set up art commissions as part of a more general interest in urban planning. Usually the budgets were very small (no more than a few thousand dollars), but the institutions had authority to commission public improvements and artworks. In some cases, such as Chicago, these institutions provided independent support for the arts as well.[67]

The Progressive Era gave momentum to this movement. Chicago established the first municipally supported art collection (later discontinued) in 1914. In 1915 Baltimore was the first American city to have a municipally supported orchestra. The Detroit Museum of Art was turned over to the city in 1919, in return for a new building. Philadelphia made the first American municipal opera grant in 1923. Between 1870 and 1910, local and state governments accounted for 40 percent of the funds available for museum building. By 1930 municipalities were spending $2.5 million a year on art museums.[68]

New York City's support for the arts dates from nineteenth-century commissions of public sculptures. In the 1890s a formal New York Art Commission was founded, to oversee the attractiveness of public buildings and parks. Yet the city already had played roles in such institutions as the Metropolitan Museum of Art, the New York Public Library, and the Brooklyn Museum of Art, as early as the 1860s. In the case of the Met, for instance, the city supplied municipal property for its construction, paid for construction, paid a sum toward maintenance, and financed some of the sculptures on Met grounds. The city government was and remains heavily represented on the Met's board of trustees.[69]

Urban involvement in the arts grew steadily, especially after World War II. Many American cities devoted more attention to tourism and decided to expand their presence as regional arts centers. These governments took greater interest in subsidizing museums, art spaces, art centers, historic buildings and neighborhoods, stadiums, and symphony orchestras.

City-level expenditures tend to be volatile, depending on economic conditions. In 2001 the New York City government allocated $162.4 million on capital spending for cultural institutions, considerably more than the entire NEA budget. This was historically a very high sum, as it had been only $20.9 million the year before. Another large leap, to $599.7 million, had been budgeted for 2002, although the economic aftermath of the terrorist attacks led to significant cuts. The main New York City funding agency is the Department of Cultural Affairs; in 2004 this agency funded the arts at a level of $118.8 million.[70]

This information puts the NEA in proper context. Once we take away the block grants to state and local agencies (40 percent of the budget), the real NEA is small relative to other sources of public arts support. Even if we take the most modest estimate possible for non-NEA sources (ignoring, for instance, many military arts programs, where finding exact data is problematic), NEA direct expenditures account for less than 10 percent of total direct governmental support for the arts in the United States.

## International Subsidies

European governments subsidize Americans' consumption of art. Many American tourists visit Europe to consume high culture, typically of a subsidized variety. Americans also buy subsidized European artistic products, such as opera recordings. Many American singers, dancers, and musicians earn all or part of their living in European markets. Richard Harrell, director of the San Francisco Opera Center, remarked: "You can't make a good living singing only in America."[71]

An American opera singer typically spends at least half the year in Europe, given the far greater number of productions and companies there. It is estimated that more opera is performed in the German-speaking world on any given night than in the rest of the world put together, owing in part to heavy subsidies. In the western part of Germany alone, more than eighty opera houses have full-time seasons. In most American houses, in contrast, only a few operas are staged a year. Even the Met has a season of less than eight months, shorter than the season in a typical provincial German opera house. In German opera houses, 50 percent of the singers employed are American; these houses thus comprise a significant portion of the demand for American singing talent.[72]

If not for European subsidies, many American creative artists would have to give up their careers. In addition to opera singers, American painters sell their pictures to subsidized European museums and American jazz musicians play at subsidized summer jazz festivals, to name two other examples of many. European subsidies bid up the wages of artists, and in that regard they force American cultural consumers to pay higher prices at home. But European subsidies also help American artists reach greater heights of creative achievement, and give American audiences access to a greater menu of choices.

Just as Americans benefit from European subsidies, European consumers benefit from American commercialism. America, by using relatively few direct subsidies, induces its cultural industries to look toward broader commercial markets. Relative to western Europe, the United States fares worse in producing live performance of the classics; at the same time it fares better in producing electronic reproductions, such as popular-music CDs and movies. Electronic reproductions, of course, can be transported and traded easily. Europeans therefore trade for mobile American products while enjoying live opera and theater close to home.

The Europeans, in fact, probably benefit from the symbiosis more than the Americans do. The American offerings, embodied in electronically reproducible forms, are especially easy to ship to Europe. The European specialization in live performance is costlier to transport to America. Such performances can be recorded, or the artists sent on tour, but often the American tourist must instead come to Europe. The cross-Atlantic cultural symbiosis therefore does most for the European common man and for the American wealthy, educated elite. The European elite and the American common man benefit less, and those are precisely the individuals most skeptical of globalization. We have the further irony that the country accused of cultural imperialism—in this case the United States—is the place that is lacking something at home.

If the United States became more like Europe, and relied more on direct subsidies, European consumers would be among the greatest losers. American culture would be less commercial, and thus less mobile across space. Even if we believe that more direct subsidies might be good for the United States, all things considered, we should hesitate before instituting them. We should also consider the well-being of Europeans and other non-Americans. Non-Americans benefit most when the U.S. system *differs* from the other systems found around the world.

Many international cultural synergies are indirect. Hollywood often hires European "auteurs"—Luc Besson and Paul Verhoeven being prominent examples—once those directors have proven themselves in foreign markets. The auteur films may not turn a commercial profit, but European subsidies often support greater directorial independence, thus allowing the auteurs to demonstrate their talents. In other words, Hollywood uses European cinema as a training ground for talent, which it then hires on the cheap. For all its past complaints about European subsidies and "unfair competition," Hollywood benefits from those subsidies. First the subsidies keep the European filmmakers commercially weak and limit their threat to Hollywood. Second, and more important for this context, the subsidies allow European cinema to serve as a research and development laboratory for Hollywood.[73]

For these reasons, the funding policies of a single country cannot be evaluated properly in isolation from the international context. We should not think of "the American model" *versus* "the European model." Rather the world has one integrated model that combines beneficial features of both systems, and others as well. Variation in arts funding policies, and variation in social conditions more generally, supports diversity in a globalized world.[74]


## Direct Subsidies:
## Searching for Models of Success


A government-funding success story is the European "public-sector aristocracy" from the Renaissance through the nineteenth century or so. It is difficult to encapsulate several centuries of European experience, but essentially private nobles or aristocrats spent government dollars on their personal artistic projects. Sometimes they spent from the public treasury and other times they spent their private fortunes, often accumulated through government service. This system supported Titian, Poussin, Mozart, and Beethoven, to varying degrees. Under this system European monarchs and nobles acted as another customer, patron, or employer, rather than as a bureaucracy with a public mandate. They pursued their own selfish interests, rather than the common good, but in the process they supported many masterworks.[75]

In essence we want government to rely on unusual or idiosyncratic mechanisms for deciding which creative acts to support. Philip IV of Spain adhered to an idiosyncratic standard for supporting the arts: he funded whatever he liked. Philip supported many artistic losers, but he also was the primary patron of Velázquez, one of the greatest painters of all time. Velázquez's eighty-one portraits of Philip indicate the measure of support. Of course many other kings supported only hack court artists.[76]

Congressman Trent Lott from Mississippi, a critic of the NEA, unintentionally hit on a profound truth when he told John Frohnmayer (then head of the NEA), "I want you to put a redneck on those panels. . . . I'm a redneck and I want representation." In the twentieth century it was "rednecks" who drove the early development of rock and roll. At first rock received few other sources of support, besides a few independent record labels and their redneck customers. In other words, the rednecks of the 1950s outperformed many of the music critics of their time, and outperformed systems of peer review.[77]

In the abstract, government spending on the arts would have the greatest chance of succeeding if it were in the hands of crazed visionaries who remained unaccountable to the general public or to the other branches of government. Such institutions, however, are impossible in most modern democracies. Politicians would not be allowed such privileges, and they would be made accountable for their art buying. Each purchase would be the subject of potential media scrutiny. Art buying would end up as a kind of political advertisement.

This hypothetical option nonetheless provides an account of why we will never be fully happy with direct subsidies in a democratic society. Ideally arts funding should replicate the artistic benefits of a politically privileged class but without the concomitant costs. We would like our arts bureaucracy to deliver the benefits of aristocratic spending while remaining accountable within a larger bureaucracy, governed by the rule of law.

The difficulty of this task is the fundamental problem with direct subsidies. Most direct subsidies, the CIA aside, are chained to a respectable, consensually based system of democratic government. The more directly artistic their mandate, the more subsidy-granting bodies must build a broad political coalition of support. This requires them to distribute goodies widely to the artistic powers that be and limits their effectiveness as venture capitalists. At least in theory, the NEA and other bodies are to act as agents of the people rather than as private customers. They are not supposed to be preferential, unfair, idiosyncratic, and sometimes obtuse—all of which are characteristics of the selfish customers who support the diversity of commercial art markets.

The historic successes of European aristocratic arts funding thus do not provide an applicable model for direct arts funding in a contemporary democracy. In the modern world, the question is not how to elevate aristocratic taste but, again, how to encourage decentralization in a well-funded, competitive environment.

In terms of producing prestige, American arts policy has had only limited success. Most forms of non-NEA direct support attract little public attention and generate little or no prestige.

The more visible programs have occasioned as much controversy as prestige satisfaction. More generally, many individuals, especially in the United States, enjoy living under a regime where government does *not* provide much direct support to the arts. Government involvement brings negative prestige to these individuals, perhaps because it reminds them of socialism, or forces them to identify the arts with government bureaucracy. Polls on this issue indicate mixed results; while most polls show a majority of the American public in support of arts subsidies, this majority does not typically exceed 60 percent, and sometimes pollsters do not find a majority in support. The right-wing and populist objections to the NEA are well known. Whether those objections be right or wrong, their very existence weighs against the prestige argument.[78]

In terms of decentralization, the WPA has been the biggest success in the history of American arts policy. The WPA supported decentralization by giving money to unemployed artists. Virtually by definition, no one else was giving much funding or support to unemployed artists (if so, they would not have been unemployed). This principle of distribution is no guarantee of success, but it did at least make success possible or more likely, and indeed the WPA did pick a large number of future winners.

The NEA, in contrast, has moved away from its venture capitalist role, which it never fully embraced in the first place, and has become increasingly conservative. By law the NEA cannot cover more than 50 percent of a project's costs, and typically it covers no more than 10 percent. (This provision is sometimes referred to as "matching funds," although that phrase is misleading. The provision caps the total size of support but without requiring explicit leverage or matching funds.) The NEA therefore provides marginal funding to projects that probably would have existed anyway.[79]

Nor is the NEA allowed to support for-profit proposals, which further limits its ability to encourage innovation. If we look at the notable European aristocratic funders of times past, typically they supported whatever they liked, and made no distinction between for-profit and nonprofit realms.

Since 1996, the agency has not been allowed to make grants to individual artists but only to artistic institutions (except for a small number of literature and "American Jazz Master" grants). An individual artist, by definition, operates according to the logic of a for-profit, keeping whatever is earned. Furthermore a single NEA grant can easily make a difference to a single individual, whose operations are typically small in financial scope. By restricting funding to nonprofit arts institutions, the NEA has been forced to invest more heavily in the staff and bureaucracy of the art world, rather than in encouraging individual creativity.

The nature of NEA panels changed dramatically during the Nixon administration. Before that time the panels were dominated by a small number of individuals, usually artists, who took direct responsibility for choosing the best talent from the next generation. Applications were not required. Nixon, however, believed that he lacked support from America's cultural and intellectual communities, and set out to remedy this deficiency. He multiplied the NEA budget eightfold (from $8 to $64 million) and turned the NEA into a political grab bag, intended to satisfy as many cultural constituencies as possible. The quality of the grants declined accordingly. The NEA director during this era, Nancy Hanks, was extremely effective in generating congressional support, but at the expense of turning the NEA into an agency determined to seek political popularity. The bureaucratic nature of the NEA dates from this era as well. In 1967 the NEA gave away sixteen grant dollars for every dollar it spent on administration, an enviable percentage. By 1996 the NEA gave only four grant dollars for every dollar spent on administration.[80]

In 1996 Congress required that six congressional representatives (then out of a total of twenty-six, now out of a total of fourteen) sit on the National Council on the Arts, which oversees NEA decisions. Their oversight takes power away from the arts professionals that run the peer panels and makes the agency more responsive to political pressures.

By statute 40 percent of NEA funds go to state and regional arts agencies in the form of block grants. This number has risen from 20 percent to 35 percent up to its current level of 40 percent. The state and regional agencies, however, tend to be at least as conservative as the NEA; they also are regulated by overall NEA guidelines, such as the antiobscenity Helms amendment of 1991. The NEA also has faced increasing pressure to spread its expenditures regionally, whether appropriate or not, to win the support of members of Congress from the smaller states.[81]

Many of the recipient institutions already receive significant private-sector support, and some are downright wealthy or on sounder financial footing than the NEA. New York City's Metropolitan Museum of Art commonly has a yearly income greater than that of the NEA, not to mention its extraordinary endowment of paintings, valued in the billions, and its Central Park real estate. The Art Institute of Chicago takes in $96 million a year, again with a rich endowment of paintings. A large opera company or symphony might have a yearly budget in the range of $30 to $40 million. These same institutions commonly receive more than $100,000 a year apiece from the NEA, despite having access to a donor network of unparalleled wealth and generosity, as well as having talented development teams.[82]

The NEA record as a venture capitalist does include some successes. The agency provided early support for comedian Garrison Keillor's *Prairie Home Companion* on Minnesota Public Radio and funded John Irving's *World According to Garp*. In 1990, all four Pulitzer Prize winners received NEA funds at important points in their careers; the four are Mel Powell (music), Oscar Hijuelos (fiction), Charles Simic (poetry), and August Wilson (drama). The Dance Theater of Harlem, which went on to international success, was first funded under a grant from the NEA; most generally dance has probably received the biggest boost from NEA expenditures. The Vietnam War Memorial, now considered a classic of both art and historical memory, resulted from an NEA design competition. Dale Chihuly, arguably the most successful glass artist in the world, founded his Pilchuk Glass Center in part with an NEA grant.[83]

Successes become harder to find, however, once the NEA could no longer make significant grants to individual artists and could no longer support controversial projects. Congressional support for NEA autonomy is weak, requiring only a few shifts in voter sentiment to be overturned. The history of the Helms amendment, which forbade government support for "obscene" works, is instructive in this regard. When Jesse Helms first introduced the amendment in 1989, it failed in the House of Representatives by a vote of 53 to 264. In 1991, only two years and a month later, the same amendment passed by 286 to 135, primarily because of public "scandals" about what the NEA was supporting.[84]

The politics of arts funding in the United States differs greatly from that of western Europe. European governments allow artists to "capture" the grants-generating process and control it for their own ends, in return for political support. Artists have more influence over public opinion in Europe, and thus they are courted to a greater degree. Furthermore the western European citizenries are less overtly puritanical, and they do not fear artworks with controversial references to sex and religion. The American reaction to the Mapplethorpe subsidy would not have happened in the Netherlands, Sweden, Germany, or France. European arts agencies therefore have more autonomy. In contrast to the politics of art funding in Europe, American politics has not allowed artists to capture the grants-generating process at the funding agencies. The NEA uses peer review, but the peers realize they must meet guidelines or they will be overruled by the agency or eventually by Congress. NEA grants have been directed predominantly toward the artistic establishment, or toward noncontroversial educational and outreach programs, and less often toward encouraging new ideas.

We should not "blame" the NEA for its conservatism, but the tendency is difficult to avoid. The course of events represents a common fate of a subsidy-granting body in the American art world. The presence of money, and the desire to win office, implies that subsidy-granting bodies usually will be pushed to serve political rather than artistic ends. In the current American context this means conservatism, in the literal rather than the political sense. America's greatest successes with direct funding—the WPA and some of the Cold War outreach programs—show the same politicization and indeed were founded on that premise. Nonetheless they worked because their nonartistic goals overlapped with good art as a matter of luck rather than design.

Ironically one of the most convincing arguments *against* government funding comes from subsidy *advocates*, not subsidy critics. It is commonly noted that each dollar of NEA spending brings in about ten dollars of private money.[85] First, this claim may not be true, as it has not received scholarly support. But if it were true, perhaps it would be bad news. It has not been shown that the NEA draws new funds, rather than redirecting arts money from one to source to another. While NEA advocates mean to make their agency sound good, in fact they raise the specter of an excessive centralization of taste and influence. We do not necessarily want a governmental seal of approval, granted partly for political reasons, to direct large quantities of private funding.

Nineteenth-century French history provides a worst-case scenario for how taste centralization can hold back the arts. The French government at that time tried to run the art world through the government-controlled French Academy and the Salon exhibitions. Even private institutions, for much of the nineteenth century, followed the lead of government-sponsored taste. The French cultural blossoming of the late nineteenth century occurred outside the network of government-funded art and government-supported academies. Creators such as

Zola, Manet, and the Impressionist and Post impressionist painters found government to be an opponent rather than a source of support. These creators flourished only by turning to private markets for their work.

Nor has twentieth-century French history provided a reassuring case for direct subsidies. Arguably no state in history has spent more on the arts per capita, since the 1960s, than has France. Late-twentieth-century France did not, however, attain world leadership in many artistic fields, in comparison to the nineteenth century or the prewar era. French culture has become highly bureaucratic and driven by Parisian insiders, rather than by consumers or by up-and-coming creators.

Fortunately for the United States, the worst predictions about American direct funding have not come to pass. The American government has provided financial support without destroying culture, or without making American artists pawns of the state.

The NEA spends its money to ensure its political survival. This implies scattering the money widely and spending much of it on the relatively influential artistic establishment, rather than on up-and-coming artists. The NEA tries to be all things to all people. The result is an agency that, despite some successes, is pulled in too many directions at the same time.

We shall return to the relative balance between direct and indirect subsidies in the final chapter, but in the meantime we can draw some conclusions about improving the quality of our direct subsidies, whether at the federal, state, or local level. World and U.S. history suggest that direct subsidies work best when

1. the arts agency or institution is free to experiment or otherwise be idiosyncratic;
2. we focus on producing a few artistic winners, rather than imposing accountability for each and every grant;
3. we do not try to use arts policy to make everybody, or even most people, happy.

# 4. Copyright and the Future
## of Decentralized Incentives

So far we have focused on subsidies, but the legal framework of markets is no less important for the arts. After all, many people believe that large corporations—and not government—are the true threat to decentralized American artistic creativity. So do current market institutions promote a flowering of diverse visions? And how can we expect our cultural landscape to evolve on the corporate side?

Today the biggest spur for cultural decentralization has been the Internet. Most obviously, the Internet lowers the costs of market entry. Cultural suppliers can sidestep intermediaries and reach consumers directly. For instance many artists give away free music samples or sell their product through online music services. The major music companies are losing their importance as market gatekeepers. Buyers in distant locales can order a wide range of books and CDs through Amazon.com and other online retailers. Online galleries and eBay bring together buyers and sellers in distant locales and lower information costs. Web postings give poets new outlets. Best sellers and mainstream goods and services were already widely available; the Internet has swung the relative balance toward niche items.

The Internet also serves as a publicity engine. Musical performers and groups use online services to track the interests of their fans. Fans use the services to discover new groups, or to follow groups they already like. It is now easier to buy tickets, discover concert locales, follow a celebrity, exchange music recommendations, order books, and read book reviews, all using new technologies.

Rather than articulate these well-known benefits in detail, I wish to focus on how the Internet might *threaten* financial decentralization. Specifically, the Internet makes some kinds of copyright harder to enforce. Once a cultural good is converted into digital form, it can be offered free of charge for downloading. Many copyright-protected outputs, whether in art, music, or literature, are now available on the Web, often against the express wishes of the copyright holders. The future may hold no enforceable copyright protection for many creative outputs, which raises the question of how decentralized financial incentives will continue to operate.[1]

Think of copyright as a response to the government's inability to pick artistic winners. In a first best world, a government would subsidize idea suppliers directly and reward the best ideas. Copyright would not be needed. Idea suppliers would receive higher returns without consumers having to pay higher prices. We do not, however, trust governments to do this job especially well. So we put rewards in the hands of the consumers, through copyright law. Suppliers receive copyright revenue only when they can persuade consumers to spend their money on a good or service. Copyright law and decentralized artistic finance are two sides of the same coin.

That being said, copyright represents government intervention rather than laissez-faire. It shows that the notion of government neutrality toward the arts is a chimera. In reality the system of property rights in the reproducible arts is based on government fiat. To what extent is copyright a natural protection of property rights, and to what extent is it a governmental grant of monopoly power? There is no simple answer to this question. The basic idea of copyright may have roots in natural law, but the practical application of copyright law is utilitarian, practical, and often morally arbitrary.

If copyright were based on a "moral right to the product of the human mind," it would have to be enforced far more stringently than it is today. It would be possible to copyright mathematical theorems, or the theories of relativity and quantum mechanics. Copyright would never expire, and artistic or intellectual borrowings would require payment of a fee, an unworkable system. Furthermore we deliberately seek differential enforcement of copyright. Dennis Rodman, a professional basketball player at the time, copyrighted the arrangement of tattoos on his body. At the same time we have no copyright for fashion design, textiles, calligraphic works, most forms of choreography, many kinds of craft design, and most scientific ideas. Nor do property rights in the expression of an idea protect against parody.[2]

The call for government neutrality toward the arts therefore represents an unattainable ideal. There is no well-defined starting point for property rights endowments as a baseline for defining laissez-faire. We thus return to practicality, and also direct government involvement, in the most fundamental of arts incentives, namely determining rights to revenue streams.[3]

The government's role in defining artistic property rights is far more important than its funding and subsidy decisions. Copyright law, by protecting the expression of artistic ideas, specifies who has rights to revenues and shapes decentralized arts incentives. Copyright law is especially relevant in the United States, where reproducible popular culture has flourished to an unprecedented degree. In a typical year, recorded music accounts for revenues of $11 billion, the movie industry (including TV rights) for $44 billion, and book publishing for $28 billion. These copyright revenues draw more cultural goods and services to the marketplace. They make idea generation more profitable and bring us a wider menu of cultural choices.

Given this context, I will consider how decentralized finance will likely evolve in a regime of weaker copyright enforceability. The best available evidence suggests that the virtues of the American system will remain robust. The Internet may make copyright law too hard to enforce, relative to an ideal state of affairs. Nonetheless the future is likely to be more workable than is commonly believed. We can expect artistic markets to change in fundamental ways, but the symbolic and prestige components of art will keep decentralized finance robust.

## Is Copyright Indeed Disappearing?

It is outside the scope of this book to debate the details of whether or when protection and encryption technologies will beat the hackers and copiers. Future technologies are difficult to predict. Nonetheless copyright enforceability will likely weaken within our lifetimes, if only temporarily. The most general argument is simply that technologies are changing. We cannot count on current levels of enforceability to persist.

Copyright has not been easily enforced throughout much of history. In eighteenth-century Europe, opera scores and printed manuscripts were zealously protected, often without success. Composers and publishers feared that copyists would capture profits and limit the incentives for creation. More generally, Chinese and Islamic histories show little in the way of copyright protection. Copyright was not part of their system of laws. Until modern times, the reach of law was not sufficiently far to make strict and extensive copyright enforceable.

The relative strength of copyright enforcement in the twentieth century has been a historical and technological accident. Effective copyright enforcement depends on a delicate balance of technologies, as protection abilities must outpace copying abilities. This balance is unlikely to reign continually during rapid technological change, as we are now experiencing.

We have some specific reasons to believe that the enforcement balance is turning against enforceable copyright. The decoding of digital information into output requires decryption. We can think of a DVD disc as "decrypted" by the DVD player whenever the movie is shown. A CD is decrypted when it is played and the digital stream of information is converted into music. In principle a hacker needs only to intercept this stream of information. If nothing else, the CD can be taped in analog format and the information can be reconverted into digital form. Any cultural output that can be copied and delivered to many consumers can also be made available on the Internet for free.

The static nature of the target makes illegal copying hard to prevent. Encrypted material sits around for years, and the supplier has only one chance to opt for a protection technology. That technology, once in place, is a fixed target. Sooner or later hackers are likely to succeed, just as a Norwegian teenager posted the code for how to copy DVD discs. It is then only a matter of time before the "back catalogs" of many cultural genres become freely available. In other words, the hackers need to win only once to achieve a permanent victory, at least for previously issued materials.

Some cultural producers have brought lawsuits against the institutions that aid Internet-based copying. Current legal campaigns appear to have deterred many would-be downloaders. Nonetheless the illegal exchange of copyright-protected material has not ceased. File-sharing services can come from beyond the reach of United States law, or in the future they may offer anonymity for their users. Furthermore the American public has only a limited appetite for lawsuits against file sharers, most of whom do not resemble common criminals.

Finally, the entire war against illegal file-sharing may be a red herring. New technologies use software to scan satellite radio stations and identify desired songs. The software then makes a copy of the music for the listener, in completely legal fashion. Simply by turning on the software an individual can, over the course of a few months, obtain just about any well-known song he wants. If illegal file-sharing were truly stopped, some version of this idea likely would arise to take its place.

So do we face the prospect of a world where creative artists cannot collect payment for their labors? Will consumers find that the supply of new culture is no longer forthcoming? Will the Internet, and by implication American telecommunications policy, force American popular culture into bankruptcy and overturn financial decentralization?

## Love of Symbols

To see how the future will likely evolve, let us turn to the symbolic nature of culture. Buyers crave not only material goods and services but also symbols. I define a symbolic good as offering a feeling or perception of affiliation. A teenager may go to a Madonna concert to express her solidarity with feminism. Rich yuppie lawyers collect contemporary art to look "cool." Social climbers go to the opera to be seen. Our cultural decisions tell the rest of the world what kind of person we are or at least what kind of person we are pretending to be. Buying culture is about identity and pride. Of course the relevant audience often includes *ourselves*. Most people want to think of themselves as a certain kind of person. They use art toward this end, even if they must self-deceive to do so.[4]

As copyright becomes harder to enforce, suppliers will reap less revenue from selling concrete products, and will reap more revenue from selling associated symbolic goods. They will convert cultural ideas into forms that cannot be reproduced so easily over the Internet. They will sell "the book-buying experience at a superstore," to name one possibility.

Demands for cultural symbols will remain robust even when copyright protection for the accompanying cultural expressions is weak. The Internet transmits many cultural products very well, but it cannot copy most of the associated symbolic values with equal facility. The Internet does offer its own symbolic values, such as a certain idea of "technological cool," but rarely do these symbolic values exactly copy non-Internet symbolic values. So we should not think of the Internet as selling the same cultural products but at lower prices. More accurately the Internet is offering a different set of products altogether, most of all in the symbolic realm. When viewed in these terms, it is easier to see why reproducible culture will survive the online revolution.

The book trade shows the importance of symbolic demands. To put it bluntly, most people do not read the books they buy. In January 2000 Marcel Proust's *Remembrance of Things Past* was number 544 on the U.K. best-seller list, yet few of its buyers finish a single volume. Many of them never start the book. Highbrow best sellers by authors such as Stephen Hawking and Camille Paglia are read by only a small fraction of their purchasers. Most cookbooks are never used. Popular-fiction best sellers and self-help books are widely read, but much of the book trade is about selling image and symbols, rather than words on paper.[5]

Nonreading buyers are not always wasting their money out of stupidity, as an elitist perspective might suggest. Rather most people buy books for reasons other than the desire to process the information. People buy books to put them on the coffee table, to show their friends, or as a measure of expressive support for some idea or celebrity. Buying a book bears some resemblance to individual voting, rooting for a sports team, or donating to a charity. Perhaps most of all, people buy books to support their self-image as a kind of person who likes a certain kind of book. For these reasons, books as we know them will not go away anytime soon. Book superstores have recognized this fact, and they offer the book-buying experience, replete with Starbucks coffee, singles night, live concerts, high ceilings, stylish interiors, and celebrity lectures. Superstores have increased the symbolic values associated with book shopping, and in a manner that digital technologies and the Internet cannot easily replicate.

When people care primarily about information, practicality and cheap access matter most. Then the Internet will triumph. The Internet is ideal for retrieving stock price quotes or serving as an encyclopedia. The *Encyclopedia Britannica* no longer is put out in physical form, and the Web itself serves as a giant searchable encyclopedia. But in most spheres of reading, most people do not care if the Internet puts all the world's texts at their fingertips for free. They did not want to read much in the first place. They do not care if Saint Thomas's *Summa Theologae*, 652 pages in a regular print edition, can be found for free on the Web.[6]

One of the biggest early web successes in the book market came when 400,000 people downloaded Stephen King's *Riding the Bullet* in the first twenty-four hours it was available. Yet most of these people appear to have taken more interest in the downloading experience, and participating in a new trend, than in reading the work. One industry source estimated that three-quarters of the downloaders did not read the book.[7]

The symbolic nature of book ownership and purchase helps the book trade compete with free public libraries. Libraries already offer readers free access to many or perhaps most of the books they would like to read. And to the extent that libraries are incomplete, this is the result of patron choices or at least patron indifference; if would-be readers and taxpayers pressured public libraries, they could change book-ordering policies. Yet the free public library does not put the book trade out of business. Books must be returned to the library within three weeks, and the library "book experience" is usually lacking in glamor. The book trade can coexist with freely available book copies, provided the booksellers bundle their wares with attractive symbols and appealing complementary experiences.

So let us step back and sum up how this market works. Most customers care about the symbolic goods more than the information embodied in the cultural product. Large numbers of books are produced, and the market favors books that are easily packaged with complementary symbols. Dedicated readers reap an enormous cross-subsidy, but they are relatively small in number. The system also protects the creative freedom of many authors. If all book buyers were to read what they bought, publishers would pressure writers to serve these would-be readers. Instead writers can enjoy greater latitude, at least provided they can offer up some complementary symbolic goods. Writers must instead write books that people will pretend to want to read. On all sides we see an uneasy albeit workable cultural truce, shored up by the demand for symbolic values.

## Which Institutions Best Produce Symbols and Aura?

For decentralized finance to succeed, legitimate suppliers must be able to sell some relevant symbols more effectively than rogue hackers can. The for-profit production of reproducible popular culture will then remain profitable, precisely because people are willing to pay for symbols and their associated aura.

There is of course no guarantee that legal suppliers will offer more desirable symbolic goods. Internet suppliers, whether legal or not, compete to supply symbolic consumption just as they compete in terms of product and information transmission. Many Web sites make cultural consumption a deeper and more interesting experience, or at least try to do so. Cultural Web sites may greet us with the image of a beautiful painting, a fanfare of trumpets, or the whiff of a pleasing scent. We can think of these symbols as producing an aura. In the case of online music, many young people enjoy the "outlaw" image of capturing copyrighted music from large corporate conglomerates. The very name "Napster" suggested something deliciously conniving.

Most legitimate cultural suppliers, however, offer unique forms of aura that hackers and outlaw Web sites cannot replicate. Internet auras differ by the very nature of computer technology. No matter how good the Web site, looking at pictures over the Internet is not like being in a museum. So while Internet-based and non-Internet forms of aura will compete, the Internet-based auras will not win in every case. More plausibly, two distinct networks will arise.

The two forms of aura often prove to be complements. That is, looking at pictures over the Internet, and enjoying the concomitant Internet-based aura, may interest viewers in finding out what a real museum is like. Similarly, people may be keener to buy books if they can use their home pages to tell others what they have read. Online music, even if it lowers CD sales, may encourage fans to see more concerts. And so on. These complementarities are no accident; rather each medium will evolve to free ride on and match the symbolic goods offered by the other medium.

That being said, legal product suppliers hold some key advantages in producing certain kinds of aura. Aura often comes through the association of a product with given institutions, given celebrities, or a given history. This favors products supplied by identifiable institutions with well-established reputations. Book superstores, concert halls, and art museums have auras because institutions have invested resources in making their venues attractive, interesting, or otherwise focal. Outlaw or hacker suppliers, who wish to remain anonymous or at least low profile, are unlikely to make comparable investments. They cannot easily turn aura-producing investments into reputational or financial gains for themselves.

In other words, customers often do not want products supplied by anonymous institutions. This truth limits the dangers from copyright-damaging Web sites. If the copyright-damaging institution is truly anonymous, and thus impervious to legal sanction, it will have a hard time producing aura. Other copyright-infringing institutions have a central and traceable identity and thus can develop aura more easily and effectively. These same institutions, however, usually can be reached by the law.

Individuals who download culture from the Internet are akin to those who buy their products wholesale rather than paying higher retail prices. They are cutting out the middleman, which in this case happens to include the artist as well. Wholesale purchases exist in many markets, and they do constrain the level of retail prices. Nonetheless it is rare for wholesale purchases to destroy a retail market altogether. Typically many customers are willing to pay extra for services of packaging, presentation, selection, and aura. The existence of wholesale furniture outlets does not put department stores out of the furniture business, even though the price differential is often a large one. For similar reasons, the Internet will not bankrupt cultural industries, though it is changing how they do business.

As competition from the Internet intensifies, cultural suppliers will have to invest more intensely in nonreproducible forms of aura. The Russian composer Scriabin prophesied that the music of the future would be a live, multisense experience, involving not only sound but also images, a communal atmosphere, and even smell. He was the first prophet of the drug-soaked "rave," a contemporary phenomenon in the world of electronic music. Scriabin also pointed out, unwittingly, the direction of live culture in an Internet age.

Ironically the Internet will make much of our culture more "primitive," more visceral, and more orgiastic. As copyright protection weakens, cultural suppliers will move into areas that digital hackers cannot "steal." This will likely involve live entertainment, public spectacles, and remarkable, once-in-a-lifetime experiences. Culture will become more thrilling, and more like the cultures of ancient societies, such as the live theater or pagan rituals of ancient Greece. For-profit culture will move away from the mere transmission of information and will become increasingly invested with nonreproducible aura. The emotional force of Haitian voodoo ceremonies, replete with trances, wild dancing, and live animal sacrifice, cannot be replicated online.

These trends were in place even before illegal file-sharing became popular. Live theater is more popular today than twenty years ago. Live raves and techno concerts offer musical experiences—replete with dance and drugs—that cannot be reproduced very well on disc. The

United States is in the midst of a museum boom. Attendance is rising, and museums are increasingly important public spaces, community symbols, and architectural masterpieces. "Historical reenactments" are not exactly culture in the narrow sense. Nonetheless they provide another example of the rising interest in the exciting live experience, even when reproducible culture is more available than ever before.

## What About Recorded Music?

The problem of Internet copying is most serious when artistic products involve little or no aura. The consumption of recorded music, for instance, involves few complementary goods from the supplier, except perhaps for the album cover and liner notes. Consumers simply sit at home and pop a compact disc into a stereo. Music downloads come close to replicating this basic experience. The relevant symbolic complements, be they smoking pot or dancing in one's living room, are added by the consumer and do not come from the music company. So if the illicit musical product is available, how will musicians continue to earn a living?

First, illegal downloading is unlikely to eliminate material music products such as CDs and DVDs. Many individuals find computers and online music to be inconvenient or intimidating. While it is easy to predict that these cultural barriers will fall away, we are not close to this point in time. For most Americans, circa 2005, buying music in the store remains the easiest way to get it. Furthermore illegally shared files do not give equivalent sound quality, at least for the time being. Again, it is easy to proclaim that technology will remedy these shortcomings. But who would have expected that digital technologies, especially the mp3 file, would have lowered music quality to a level below that of many old 78s? For the foreseeable future, online music will be better in some ways and worse in others.

That being said, online music may cause music company revenues to fall significantly. Online competition will constrain music companies and limit their pricing options.

Some CDs will become more expensive. In economic terminology, online music may drain off the "elastic" segment of market demand, the segment most responsive to changes in price. The remaining buyers may be richer, busier, older, less computer-literate, or somehow less able to shop around. These buyers might be more willing to pay higher prices. Since those who would rebel against the higher price have already left the market, price might go up. Furthermore music companies sometimes charge low prices in the hopes of generating a snowball of fan interest in their product. If the natural market base is smaller, this motive for low prices will go away. Note that specialty CD issues usually have higher prices than very popular CDs.

At the same time other CDs will become cheaper. In these cases we are closer to the example of the videocassette, for which the possibility of (illicit) copying lowers prices for everyone. When a large pool of potential buyers remain in the market, even in light of copying opportunities, the supplier will try to capture those buyers by lowering price and expanding volume. Some new CDs might cost only a few dollars rather than almost $20.

Most likely, some CDs will become cheaper and others more expensive. But under either case—rising prices or lower prices—Internet competition will cut into the revenues of the music industry and reshape our cultural networks.

## Marketing and Talent Selection: What Would We Lose?

Most musical artists (99.97 percent, by one estimate) earn little or nothing from the sale of their recordings and thus earn little or nothing from musical copyright.[8] Instead these artists usually make their living, if they make a living at all, by giving concerts. But we should not be fooled by these facts. The diminution of copyright income would affect the entire music industry, including these performers.

Music companies do not know who will be the next big stars. So they invest in a large number of musicians, not knowing what will hit.

They lose money on most of their investments and profit only from a relatively small number of significant winners. Of the 30,000 CDs released in the United States in 2002, only 404 sold more than one hundred thousand copies. Twenty-five thousand of the releases sold fewer than a thousand copies.[9]

It is the prospect of finding new stars that motivates the music companies to take chances on unknown artists. The economic problem is not only to get revenues to the artist, in return for music. We also must get other parties, such as entertainment companies, to invest in new artists and give them a chance to reach consumers.

Smaller returns to the megastars will mean that music companies will invest fewer resources across the board. Many midlevel artists will suffer as a result. If we examine a typical modern recording contract, an artist receives about 12 to 13 percent royalties for each compact disc sold.[10] So if a compact disc sells for $16.99, the artist is receiving less than $2.00 for that disc. But the artist never sees this money in most cases. Musicians typically owe previously accumulated "debts" to their music companies for recording and promotion costs. The debts from unsuccessful releases typically are set off against their next recording. These debts need not be paid off if the performer stops recording, but they do transfer from one release to the next.

Without the gross copyright revenue flowing to the music company, most artists would be out of business after a single unsuccessful release, or could not have afforded the initial release in the first place. So even if artists see no copyright revenue, it keeps them out of debt. It is naïve to view copyright as an institution that benefits only the major entertainment corporations and a few megastars. If that were the case, significant parts of the music industry would have voluntarily abandoned copyright protection a long time ago. Some firms would have signed up musicians on cheaper terms and placed the relevant outputs within the public domain. But few hit songs if any receive this treatment, if only because both the musicians and the company need to cover their capital costs.

In reality, the music company serves as a combination of venture capitalist and banker. Companies advance money to the most favorable musical prospects in return for a share of the profits. The diminution of copyright revenue resembles a tax on financial intermediation, but in this case focused on the entertainment industry.

Without copyright, music companies would invest less in expensive studio time and would substitute cheaper technologies. In some cases music would become more immediate and less technologically re- fined. Classical CDs would draw more from tapings of live perfor- mances and less from expensive studio time. Many popular music per- formers would move closer to their roots, which were developed prior to the recording era. In other cases musicians would use new technolo- gies to mimic the effects of the studio. The personal computer would play a greater role in musical composition and recording, as virtually any musical sound can be created by digital means. Forms of elec- tronic music, such as techno and drum 'n' bass, already have benefited from this development. Overall more musical experiments would reach the market, owing to the publicity benefits of the Internet, but each experiment would be less capital-intensive.

As musicians invested less time in the studio, good live concerts would be easier to come by. Musical spontaneity would likely grow in market importance, relative to musical refinement as defined by studio expertise. Touring would become a more important source of musical income than it is today. Some recordings would be offered for free, pri- marily to provide advertising for future tours. Many artists would earn more concert income and less royalty income. They probably would have to work harder. Artists who did not like to perform live, or who were poor at live performance, would be penalized.

In the classical market, the entire back catalog of Beethoven, Bach, and Mozart recordings would be available for free. Internet users al- ready can download recordings by the great conductors and pianists of the past. In this environment it would be harder to justify a new studio-performed cycle of Beethoven symphonies. It is already the case that high-quality historic reissues, priced at budget levels, have severely damaged the market for new recordings by contemporary or- chestras. We therefore can expect the market for new studio record- ings of old works to continue to diminish, given that close substitutes are available for free. Nonetheless live concerts may be recorded and posted on the Internet for very low cost. So modern interpretations of

Beethoven symphonies need not disappear and in fact may skyrocket in number.

Songwriting could become a more important source of income for musicians. A songwriter is paid to the extent his or her songs are played or performed in public venues. The Internet does not make this form of copyright law any harder to enforce. Musical artists therefore would write their own material to an increasing degree, to try to capture these gains.

Most likely marketing expenditures would fall, and recordings would have to generate their own publicity to a greater extent. Music companies would take fewer chances on recording artists, but this does not mean that recording artists would have fewer chances to make it. The same mechanism that makes copyright income harder to capture—the Internet—can lower the costs of sorting and evaluating talent. To give a simple example, a music company executive can listen to downloads instead of sending talent scouts around to live concerts in bars and clubs.

The Internet and word of mouth are assuming greater prominence in making records popular and spreading information about their quality. Over time we can expect such "volunteer" means of producing evaluations to become more important. The sorting function of the major entertainment companies thus would be replaced by a more decentralized set of gatekeepers. On one hand, many of the new decentralized gatekeepers will not have the same profit incentive as the record companies to make accurate evaluations. These new sorters will offer opinions without regard for profit-and-loss consequences. On the other hand, the more decentralized gatekeepers will have access to a greater diversity of opinion and information. Fans will rely more on the opinions of other fans, rather than on record company forecasts of fan opinion. We would expect a greater diversity of critical opinion and a greater diversity of publicity.

Most of the costs incurred by a music company stem from finding, evaluating, recording, and promoting musical talent. If a given bundle of music brings in less revenue, many of these costs have to be covered in some other fashion or removed from the music company, or the costly activities must be discontinued altogether.[11]

Sorting is already moving outside the entertainment companies. In some cases fans download the music and then buy over the Internet. Or a star may maintain a home page. Todd Rundgren, a rock star from the 1970s, sends his fans regular shipments of music in return for a subscription fee. In essence Rundgren did the sorting and finding for his fans, and they are willing to pay him for those services, not just for the music.[12] Digital satellite radio, another new technology, has an entire station devoted to bands without recording contracts.

The Internet will continue to bring new means of performing the sorting functions. Just as Google.com sorts Web pages, so can information technology sort songs and albums on the basis of popularity or other criteria. Many online file-trading services already offer versions of this idea. Amazon.com allows fans to rank CDs for all to see. Podcasting and music blogs allow every individual to act as a disk jockey, and we can easily measure popularity of a service by the number of hits. The music companies, at best, are trying to guess what fans want. The Internet allows us to measure what fans want more cheaply and effectively than ever before.

If paying the *artist* enough to get the music produced is the relevant question (as opposed to paying the music company to do the sorting), Internet music faces a relatively low threshold. Even if the song price is lower, the artist may reap a higher percentage of the gross (as had been the case on MP3.com). So we need not think of these services as needing to generate enough revenue to cover current CD prices. Online music makes it possible to save significant sums on retail expenses, which may run from 10 to 50 percent of the price of a CD.[13]

The nonentertainment corporate world might increase in importance as a musical gatekeeper. Companies might give away music for free, over the Internet, but "wrap" the music in an advertisement. Downloading the song might require an individual to first hear or see an advertisement. This model will be sustainable as long as the cost of experiencing the ad remains below the inconvenience of pirating the music (ad-free) from the Internet. Or the very offer of free downloads will constitute the advertisement. In this model the consumer has to go through the ad to get to the music. Alternatively the company may serve as patron to the artists, in return for free publicity.

This model takes musical promotion out of the hands of the record companies and puts it into the hands of large nonmusical corporations. The popular music sector, for all the publicity it receives, is small relative to many other sectors of the economy. Coca-Cola alone, for instance, has annual revenues almost twice as high as the entire music industry, which is closer in size to the annual revenues of Northwestern Mutual Life Insurance. In quantitative terms, it is not unrealistic to fund part of the music industry through corporate advertising revenue. American tax law, which allows advertising expenditures to be written off as a business expense, helps in this regard.[14]

Some forms of music will move into the not-for-profit sector and fund themselves with donations. Just as people give money to support their local symphony orchestra, they might give money to support their city's leading jazz band or perhaps even a rock and roll group. Some record companies might reorganize as nonprofits, or existing nonprofits could issue more recordings, as orchestras are starting to do. Donors could be asked to support the free distribution of such recordings over the Internet, just as they are now asked to pay for construction costs of a new symphony hall.

To fund an artistic activity by donation, of course, requires that the activity be surrounded by an aura of status and prestige. When opera and the symphony orchestra moved from the for-profit to the nonprofit realm in the nineteenth century, they abandoned their earlier carnival-like atmosphere and turned themselves into status clubs and networking institutions. Unable to sell their product for a profit, they instead traded reputation to their patrons, using the music as a focal point for organizing the production of status. Donations were sought to ration access to these networks, as we have seen also for museums. Insofar as other forms of music or art enter the nonprofit realm, they are likely to follow a similar path. By becoming more status-oriented, these arts will seek to provide something that the Internet cannot replicate.[15]

Overall the symbolic and informational functions of art may become increasingly separate, rather than integrated in the same products. The Internet will offer pure information, in the form of cultural "stuff," and other outlets for the arts will rely more heavily on the production and sale of symbolic goods. Just as high culture and low culture have split, consumers may put together their own cultural portfolios. To an increasing degree, consumers mix and match informational and symbolic experiences from a wide variety of genres and supply sources.

## How Should We Evaluate Music Worlds?

From the aesthetic point of view (see chapter 1), we achieve a good result to the extent the music market produces enduring masterpieces. We look to the judgment of history. In this perspective, 1968 was a great year for music because it had the Byrds' *Sweetheart of the Rodeo* and Captain Beefheart's *Safe as Milk*, even though the albums did not sell well at the time or subsequently. From today's vantage point, few people care that the average pop song of the 1960s was poorly constructed and overly sentimental. Few people downgrade the 1960s because Herman's Hermits and Herb Alpert and the Tijuana Brass sometimes pushed the Beatles and The Rolling Stones off the top of the charts. The aesthetic point of view emphasizes peaks of achievement. It refers to what lasts, rather than the typical product or whether every listener at the time was happy.

From this aesthetic point of view, the weakening of copyright enforcement should not occasion serious worry. Most critics argue that today we have too much investment in mass culture and too little in niche culture. Online music, by weakening copyright enforcement, will force marketing expenditures to fall, moving us away from mass culture and limiting the creation of megastars. To the extent that marketing costs fall, the music market will be less "winner take all," less geared toward commonly shared celebrities, and more oriented to satisfying diverse and heterogeneous niche tastes. Most critics would like this result.

We already see that megastars expect to lose the most from downloadable music. The less popular musicians typically have a more favorable attitude toward a regime of weaker copyright enforceability. The Internet, including illicit file-sharing, often provides a relative boost to musicians aiming at small and sophisticated audiences.[16]

In contrast to an aesthetic point of view, consider the preferences of consumers and the economic perspective. The most obvious benefit is that the Internet brings an incredible online "universal jukebox." The Internet takes music that is already there and distributes it to consumers more widely. Illegal file-sharing in particular brings music to people who otherwise would not pay for it.

That being said, it is difficult to judge how a given level of illegal downloads will affect economic efficiency. First, the quantity of music sold in a given year is not a very accurate indicator of how much value consumers receive from music. Fans commonly experiment by buying a number of CDs, only a few of which pay off and become favorites. Many or most of the products bought are quickly regarded as disappointments and discarded; in this regard the market for CDs differs from the market for refrigerators. With music, whether consumers like what they bought is at least as important as the absolute size of the industry.

The Internet already helps music companies track fan demands. When fans sample online music, usually they can figure out whether or not they would like the entire CD. Many of these fans still buy the CD to get better sound, to have the music in more convenient form, to receive the packaging, and so on, as discussed above. These fans usually will be happy with their purchases. As a result, it will be harder for the music companies to issue low-quality CDs. Of course this tighter monitoring of quality may cause the number of new issues to decline. In nominal terms the industry will shrink, but at the same time it may produce more real value for consumers. For this reason, a shrinking music industry, as measured in terms of either dollars or new releases, can be *desirable* from an economic point of view.

## What Do Consumers Really Want from Music?

Evaluating the efficiency consequences of illegal downloads is difficult for a more fundamental reason. Most generally, we do not understand the demand for music very well. We do not understand what most fans want from their music. Just as book buyers are not always readers, the music market is not always about the tunes. Sometimes it is about symbolic values.

It is a mystery why fans spend almost all their music money on products of very recent vintage. Until we untangle this puzzle, and we have not yet, we will not understand how Internet music is likely to affect consumer welfare.

Most consumers are not interested in buying much music from 1950, regardless of its objective quality in the eyes of the critic. Music from 1650 is even less popular. Few people search the history of music for "the best recordings" and focus their buying on those. Rather, in any given year the most recent recordings dominate the charts. At a typical moment, all the Billboard Top 40 singles, or albums, come from the most recent two years of recorded output. Every now and then there is a Beatles revival, but such events are the exception rather than the rule. Consumers evince an overwhelming preference for music produced in the very recent past.

Most likely the music market is about more than simply buying "good music," as a critic might understand that term. People buy music to signal their hipness, to participate in current trends, or to distinguish themselves from previous generations. Buyers use music to signal their social standing, whether this consists of going to the opera or listening to heavy metal. Others value partaking in novelty per se. They find newness exciting, a way of following the course of fashion, and the music market offers one handy arena for this pursuit. For some people music is an excuse to go out and mix with others, a coordination point for dancing, staying up late, drinking, or a singles scene. Along these lines, many fans seem to enjoy musical promotions, hype, and advertising as ends in themselves, and not merely as means to hearing music. They like being part of the "next big thing." The accompanying music cannot be so bad to their ears as to offend them, but the deftness of the harmonic triads is not their primary concern.

In other words, the features of the market that matter to the critic may not be very special to consumers at all. Most of all, consumers seem to care about some feature of newness and trendiness, more than they care about music per se. So how much does it matter, from a consumer's point of view, if weaker copyright protection reshapes the world of music?

Under one hypothesis, the specific musics of our day are easily replaced or, in economic terminology, highly substitutable. All other things equal, people will buy the new, but they could get along with alternatives almost as well. For instance perhaps "ravers" could use Gregorian chants to define their cultural status. Indeed one chant CD (*Chant*) had a very long and successful chart run. Young rave and techno fans were among the largest buyers of this recording.

Or perhaps half the supply of music could do almost as good a job of supplying symbolic goods, especially if music companies can track fan demand with greater facility. Alternatively, individuals could rely more heavily on alternative means, such as fashion, to signal their social standing and participate in trends. These points are all speculations, but they show the difficulty of pinning down what music fans really care about.

Consider two further examples. First, in the former Soviet Union, dissident rock and roll bands performed many popular-culture functions and commanded a fervent following. These bands fell short of the objective critical quality of their Western counterparts. Still they provided consumers with many useful services, including a means to signal rebellion against the Soviet state. Second, in 1941, the major radio stations refused to carry the catalog of the music publisher ASCAP, in a dispute over fees. At that time ASCAP, the leading music publisher and clearinghouse in the United States, dominated the music market. The stations instead played BMI music, which was more oriented toward rhythm and blues and offered less Tin Pan Alley, crooning, and big band. Radio listeners seemed to take the sudden change in stride; there is little evidence of a serious problem. Music fans continued pretty much as before, except for the change in styles and associated music publishers.[17]

For whatever reason, most consumers find it harder to reorient their attention toward older music. Perhaps only new music allows for effective signaling and sorting. When music is new, individuals can show that they are connected to current modes of thinking and feeling. Not everyone can know "what is in," because "what is in" is changing so frequently. That very fact makes it worthwhile for consumers to put effort into following the new. The music market might therefore churn product to help people communicate their identities to others, and to help people play an ongoing dynamic game of clues and cues. Furthermore previous generations already have claimed older musics, making them less well suited for social differentiation. Perhaps musical taste is a game of secession and repudiation more than anything else.

So the music of Chuck Berry "no longer fits" the world of 2005, and cannot be made to fit it. Critics still love the music, and some niche consumers will be drawn to its merits, but it can never hold the current place of Britney Spears. That is why hit reissues are rare. It is not because consumers still remember the older musics. Rather most consumers do not care about them very much. It thus appears that the value of popular music, to most consumers, consists of some temporally specific tracking quality. This may involve an ability to follow, correspond to, or perhaps even shape the spirit of the times. Rejection of the previous Zeitgeist may be part of this same process. For consumers, this tracking quality is a significant part of the value of music. The music industry is delivering the goods when its product performs this tracking function, and otherwise not.

The Internet helps music perform tracking functions of this kind. Because of its capabilities, the time period between the launch of a new group and its acceptance should decline. Music companies should be more in tune with fan tastes. More diverse groups of fans should find musics to track their respective social needs. More and better live concerts should bring customers closer to musical experience. We therefore have some reasons to be optimistic about the welfare consequences of weaker copyright enforceability from the consumer's point of view, and not just from an aesthetic point of view.


## The Visual Arts


To date the visual arts have not experienced serious copyright problems with the Internet. Many individuals post unauthorized copies of paintings and other artworks, but these copies have not disrupted the markets for the originals. The difference in market value between an original artwork, even a print, and a digital copy of that artwork remains enormous. In contrast copies of literature or recorded music are worth almost as much as the original.

We nonetheless can imagine a more distant future when digital holography, or some comparable technology, allows for the very accurate reproduction of visual artworks. In the limiting case, very accurate digital reproductions might allow viewers to enjoy their own copies of the *Mona Lisa* or of a Monet haystack painting, indistinguishable from the original to the naked eye.

This scenario, while far off, would not spell doom for the art world. First, the original may continue to be worth much more than the copies. The price difference between an original artwork and a copy, even a very good copy, is significant. Experts have been fooled many times by artistic copies, frauds, and forgeries. But once an artwork is revealed to be nonauthentic, its value plummets immediately, even though the quality of the nonauthentic work remains constant. Buyers care about the aura of the original and its symbolic value, even when they cannot tell the difference between the real and the copy. Why they feel this way is an interesting question, but the attitude seems to be robust. It will prevent copies from completely cannibalizing the market for original artworks.

If copies are good enough, perhaps the difference in value between fakes and real artworks will disappear or narrow over time. Perhaps we shun unauthorized copies of artworks because, deep down, we know they are not very good. Forgeries are devalued because, once we realize they did not come from the hand of Rembrandt or van Gogh, their weakness becomes common knowledge. The fakes then drop to the value of their true aesthetic worth or lower, for reasons of attached stigma. So if unauthorized copies were truly of high quality—as good as the original *Mona Lisa*—over time the premiums for original works might diminish. Social conventions might change. We already see that the current generation of art buyers is not so put off by the "multiple" nature of artistic photographs. In contrast the previous generation of buyers was keener to buy "original" works. If we look to the past, prestigious museums once bought and displayed copies of famous artworks, rather than focusing solely on originals (a copy of a Leonardo hangs in the Prado to this day, though as more of a curiosity than anything else).[18]

Higher values for copies would not, however, ruin the market for art. Instead the arts would become more popular and less elitist. Artists would sell many copies of a single work to a large market, rather than only a few copies to very wealthy buyers. In essence, more artists would be induced to enter the print market, albeit with a higher quality of reproduction than is currently available.

As in the music or book markets discussed above, prints would have to sell more cheaply, given the possibility of unauthorized reproduction. The price of a print could not be much above its cost of unauthorized reproduction. The relatively low profit margin would mean a smaller role for art intermediaries, such as galleries, just as online music means a smaller role for record companies. Galleries currently certify product quality, and to some extent word of mouth and volunteer Internet surveys would take over this function, analogous to the above discussion of the music market.

We could expect art school training to become less profitable, given that art copiers could mimic the efforts of art producers. Art might become more "Outsider," more "naïve," and less schooled. This mirrors how music might be forced to lower its capital costs; again, a kind of disintermediation will take place.

The effects on the art market might resemble how electronic recording reshaped the music market. Many new genres rose in visibility, such as jazz and country and western. Overall most music became more popular, making many less popular musics more viable. Artists specializing in many relatively obscure musical forms, such as free jazz, have used recording to reach a wider audience and earn a better living. Recording has brought more diversity at the fringes, while making the center of the market more profitable.

High-quality copies also would alter the symbolic values associated with painting. The visual arts currently serve as a field for producing social status and differentiation. In contrast, a reproducible genre such as popular music is more likely to serve functions of cultural bonding and coordination around popular stars. The widespread availability of good copies would lower the exclusivity of art ownership and make art easier to use as a signal of commonality, rather than as a signal of distinction. This might make art buyers more interested in very new products and less interested in the classics, again as we have found in music markets.

## Cinema

Cinema is one of the hard cases for the prospect of weaker copyright enforceability.

Theater-based cinema, which bundles informational and symbolic goods, faces little danger. Movies are about more than just seeing the film. Movies are "date movies," "family movies," and so on; they are about sharing popcorn, making fun of other people waiting in line, and simply getting out of the house. Furthermore many moviegoers are willing to pay to see the film on a large screen.

Nonetheless freely available digital DVD copies would damage business significantly. Circa 2005, Hollywood film studios receive over half of their revenue through the home video/DVD market.[19] This source of income would likely fall. Furthermore some people will wait for the free pirated digital copy at home, in lieu of going out to the theater. That is why movies are the problematic case for any fan of Internet-transmitted digital culture.

Today it is not very convenient for most home users to download copies of films, if only because it is hard to transfer them to one's television. That being said, several hundred thousand DVD copies are downloaded illegally off the Internet every day, usually through file exchange services. These copies may compete more seriously with DVDs and theatrical releases as technical obstacles diminish. We can imagine a computer-TV hookup that would download a movie while the viewer watches, with no glitches or interruptions.

Unlike live movies, videocassette or DVD rentals do not offer many complementary symbolic goods in addition to the movie itself. DVDs offer various auxiliary features, but these could be downloaded with the movie. This market therefore is vulnerable to Internet pirate copies. Even if a production company refused to release a digital copy of a film, pirate digital copies might be sneaked out of the studio or recorded in a theater. Only a single pirate copy is needed to generate widespread circulation.

The more strongly the Internet competes with movie theaters, the more theaters will invest in a nonreplicable aura. Moviegoing would become more of a live experience, and the notion of a movie theater as a "pleasure palace," prominent in the 1920s, might be revived. Perhaps the movie would somehow interact with the live experience of being there to watch it.

Movies might adapt to Internet competition, just as they survived competition from free television broadcast. As television grew popular in the 1950s and 1960s, the movie industries were devastated in the West and in Japan. It was common for movie admissions to fall by as much as a factor of five over the span of a decade or two. At the time most movies were little more than B fare, effectively "made for TV" movies on the big screen. Television took away this part of the movie market, but Hollywood responded by investing in spectacles for the large screen and expensive special effects. Today Hollywood releases fewer films per year than it did before television, owing to the migration of the "B movie" to that medium, but the industry as a whole is economically healthy.[20]

If illicit Internet copies take over the home rental market, they must compete in terms of convenience more than in terms of price. Video-cassettes have competed against illegal copies for a long time, but since it costs only $2 to rent *Raiders of the Lost Ark*, few individuals bother to make an illegal copy. The possibility of illegal copies nonetheless keeps rental prices down, forcing movie rentals into a low-price, high-volume mode. So we know that individuals are willing to pay a higher price for the legal product *if* the legal service somehow offers sufficiently greater convenience or greater product quality. This reopens the possibility that Hollywood studios will not only survive the age of digital culture but prosper in it. Exactly how and why the legal copy might offer superior convenience remains to be seen. The best-case scenario is that legal Web sites, or some form of video on demand, can outcompete illicit movie downloads. The worst-case scenario is that illegal downloads capture some share of the current DVD market. But since moviemakers apparently can prosper at low per-unit movie rental prices, we have reason to be optimistic.

## What About the Costs of Copyright?

To be sure, copyright law has its costs. Once a cultural good is produced, or if it is going to be produced in any case, copyright means that the good is distributed less widely than otherwise. To the extent information is a public good, the very best outcome distributes that information as widely as possible. In other words, once a song has been recorded, I can download it off the Internet without stopping anyone else from hearing the same song. But copyright enforcement makes information more exclusive, and more like property. All other things equal, such a protected status is undesirable for a public good.

Legislation in 1976 brought copyright protection to new extremes, namely the life of the author plus fifty years, and for a company seventy-five years from publication or one hundred years from creation, whichever is sooner. The renewal process was eliminated altogether. Over time the large corporations of the entertainment industry have captured Congress in this matter, and the copyright period has now been extended eleven times in the last forty years. The most recent extension was the Sonny Bono Copyright Term Extension Act of 1998, which expanded copyright protection to the life of the creator plus seventy years, rather than fifty. Corporate copyrights also were extended twenty years to a total of ninety-five years, as were copyrights for all works produced before 1978. The campaign to change these laws was led by Disney, which had feared the forthcoming expiration of copyright on Mickey Mouse and other lucrative cartoon characters.[21]

Copyright can restrict output in other ways as well. Many artists borrow heavily from each other, often without paying royalties or receiving permission. Disney characters are frequently drawn from European fairy tales or American folktales, without payment of any licensing fee.

Some of Bob Dylan's songs are so close to the works of Woody Guthrie that Dylan would lose a lawsuit, had Guthrie received contemporary copyright protection. Of course Guthrie borrowed heavily as well, most of all from blues musicians. This did not stop Dylan, once a populist 1960s radical, from joining the lobbying effort in favor of copyright extension.[22]

Copyright also makes it harder for rap artists to sample music. Looking back into history, many Shakespeare plays draw their plots from other works; Hamlet, for instance, was based on Thomas Kyd's *Spanish Tragedy*. Large sections of Chaucer's poetry are borrowed from other writers, through either translation or paraphrase. Blues, jazz, country music, and rap are all based on widespread borrowing of melodies and riffs, usually without any acknowledgment and certainly without any payment of licensing fees. It is debatable whether these artistic forms could have developed as we know them, had today's copyright laws been enforced all along.

That being said, these costs of copyright are easily remediable, if we so choose. We could have a copyright law establishing protections that are shorter in duration. Similarly, we could move back to earlier versions of copyright law, which prohibited outright copying but treated borrowing of ideas very liberally. So these costs of copyright, while real, do not provide a reason to throw out the entire institution.

The coming of digital culture makes current copyright laws stricter, without anyone having intended such an outcome. In previous times, the "fair use" doctrine generally gave consumers the right to make copies for their personal use. The law has not changed, but the gateways of digital culture limit consumers' real options. Lessig (2004, p. 143) explains:

> Enter the Internet—a distributed, digital network where every use of a copyrighted work produces a copy . . . because of this single, arbitrary feature of the design of a digital network, the scope of [a category of copyright law] changes dramatically. Uses that before were presumptively unregulated are now presumptively regulated. . . . let's be very specific to make this general point clear. Before the

Internet, if you purchased a book and read it ten times, there would be no plausible *copyright*-related argument that the copyright owner could make to control that use of her book. . . . But the same book as an e-book is effectively governed by a different set of rules. Now if the copyright owner says you may read the book only once or only once a month, then *copyright law* would aid the copyright owner in exercising this degree of control, because of the accidental feature of copyright law that triggers its applications upon there being a copy.

While Lessig's point is well-taken, these costs of copyright are unlikely to prove significant in the long run. Provided we can maintain decentralization of supply, copyright owners are unlikely to exert an excessively high degree of control over users. Consider, for instance, the choice of a legal online music service. Some services allow for extensive copying, ownership, and file transfer privileges, but others do not. Consumers weigh their privileges against price and other relevant metrics of quality. If the number of suppliers makes the market roughly competitive, we expect consumers to receive options that are satisfactory, relative to the real costs of supplying those options. This is standard microeconomic reasoning.

We also could seek to improve the market through a legal and institutional remedy. In particular we could modify current law to give people who want to make music available online access to mandatory licensing. We already apply various forms of this practice to radio, jukeboxes, department store broadcasts of music, cable retransmission of television signals, or to individuals who wish to perform somebody else's composition live. To provide a simple example, a radio station can play someone's song, provided it pays an appropriate fee to the copyright owner of the composition (no payment is made to the copyright holder for the recording, who is considered to benefit from airplay). The fee is set by law, in recognition of the difficulty of negotiating an appropriate price in each and every case. Similarly, we could require compulsory licensing for music over the Internet, or at least the back catalog.[23]

Today record companies have the right to withhold music from unauthorized Internet services. Compulsory licensing would require music companies to trade at a certain price. The back catalog would become immediately available to anyone willing to digitalize it. More important, online music entrepreneurs could set up on a much smaller scale. They would not need the teams of lawyers required to negotiate Internet rights with all the copyright holders. Compulsory licensing therefore would make the market in online music more competitive very rapidly.

Compulsory licensing may seem like a curious position to encounter in a book that heralds the virtues of decentralized markets. It looks like government-sanctioned price-fixing. But compulsory licensing can be given an alternative interpretation. Whatever its favorable practical effects, copyright is a government grant of monopoly. Compulsory licensing is simply forcing the monopoly holder to share some of the government-sanctioned monopoly position with others. Furthermore, the initial contractual assignments of royalty rights did not foresee the development of the Internet. Compulsory licensing is a blanket means of assigning Internet rights *ex post*. While it is highly imperfect, the other legal means of assigning these (poorly specified) rights will have problems as well.[24]

While I am an advocate of copyright in general, the current state of copyright law is neither morally nor legally sacred. Much of American musical copyright law was written for technologies of player pianos and sheet music. It was not designed for a world with Internet culture and digital reproduction. Furthermore the origins and development of copyright show a legacy of censorship, monopoly, and special privilege. In the nineteenth century the U.S. Supreme Court ruled that copyright is a statutory monopoly rather than a natural law right of the author. Going back earlier, in Renaissance Venice, the home of Western copyright law, some printers were given monopoly rights to the entire printing industry. These rights then evolved into more specific monopoly rights to print particular works; early copyright was often vested directly in the publisher, rather than the author. The subsequent development of copyright shows similarly close links to state control. Throughout much of English history, copyright law served partially as a system of censorship. The grant of a copyright was considered equivalent to a decision to allow the particular work to be published.[25]

## Whither Copyright?

In sum, the Internet and weaker copyright enforceability will have complex effects on various art worlds. The technologies are exciting, but the relevant truths are often banal. Many people will be better off while others will be worse off. The shareholders and managers of the major entertainment corporations may suffer the most. Disintermediation will occur. Many creators will be worse off, but that does not mean that the arts as a whole will suffer. Some styles will flourish while others will stagnate. Consumers are on the verge of having a universal jukebox of sorts at their disposal, granting access to the world's musical, literary, and cinematic treasures for a mere pittance. Yet most people do not care much about this marvelous opportunity. They use culture for other purposes.

When evaluating copyright enforcement, should we take the viewpoint of critics or consumers? And is the music or culture of a particular age easily replaceable or not? In neither case do we have clear answers. But none of the cases show that Internet-based digital reproduction, and weaker copyright enforceability, will bring obvious disaster to cultural markets. We can expect financial decentralization to prove robust in the future of the American arts. And the ability of large corporations to endanger that decentralization is declining over time.

We therefore should be inclined to welcome the new technologies and to enjoy and herald their benefits, rather than to restrict them by additional legal means. Furthermore we see once again that beneficial policy often arises through accident. Congress and the regulators debated telecommunications for decades and often chose ill-advised policies, such as restrictions on cable television. Yet subsidies to the Internet came with little explicit debate through the Defense Advanced Research Projects Agency (DARPA) and the Department of Defense. The Internet will go down in history as a major success for both telecommunications and culture. DARPA and the DOD likely will go down in history as the greatest benefactors our government has produced for the arts.

# 5. Toward a Beautiful and Liberal Future

Policy recommendations are problematic when values conflict. Nonetheless if I imagine myself asked to write short advice for an American presidential candidate, and forced to make the difficult judgments, I would offer the following ten points:

1. The best arts policy stimulates creative discovery more generally. This implies a strong economy, numerous and diverse sources of decentralized funding for creative enterprise, and sensible policies toward science, technology, and education. U.S. policy should not be designed to target any narrow notion of art. Many of the biggest arts policy successes are accidents. That being said, they arise from the presence of fundamentally healthy institutions. If we have good policies toward a broader notion of creative discovery, arts policy likely will be healthy as well.

2. The American system of indirect funding and support for the arts has stimulated creativity and diversity. It may not satisfy fully either the pure critic or the pure economist. Nonetheless intermediate points of view, which combine both perspectives, give the system relatively high marks.

3. In the international arena, Americans should reject the image of their country or their government as lacking in concern for the arts. The U.S. model does not elevate economy over beauty but rather helps make the two values compatible. This approach will likely create more beauty than an attempt to elevate beauty over economy.

4. The most important arts policy decisions we face today concern copyright, the Internet, and telecommunications. In these areas the very structure of property rights is up for grabs.

Whether we like it or not, we must deal with online music services that subvert current copyright law. In the long run government probably cannot stop them, short of controlling the Internet. But we need not approach the future with fear. The easy reproducibility of artistic works will have complex effects on creative labors but is unlikely to bring disaster, or overturn our ability to fund the creative arts in a decentralized manner. Nor are the current details of copyright morally sacred. The general presumption is thus to allow the free progress of technological advance. In the meantime a system of compulsory licensing fees, for online music, can improve market competition.

5. The very rationale for decentralization suggests it is difficult to provide persuasive and enduring evaluations of particular arts agencies. Instead the methods of this book are better suited to the macrolevel. Looking at individual agencies or arts appropriations would require a more careful treatment of particular aesthetic values.

6. We should take more chances with the NEA. Ideally an arts agency could identify a nascent but underfunded genre and offer support to individual artists on a relatively arbitrary and indiscriminate basis. We might make the NEA more like the New Deal's WPA. The government might pick some winners, but the money might be wasted altogether, given the difficulty of identifying appropriate booming areas.

Direct subsidies have worked best when accountability is absent, when the marketplace is failing to spot many of the best artists, and when the state can act as a strong-willed funder of idiosyncrasies. This result is not easily achieved today, when the economy has generally been healthy, commercial arts have been vigorous, politics are highly democratic, the media report government waste, and the NEA cannot easily act on whims.

7. We could improve direct subsidies. First, we could restore the full ability of the NEA to make grants to individual artists. Currently NEA funds often go to large and well-established art institutions, where they have less of a chance of making a difference.

Second, the NEA is currently reluctant to fund more than 10 percent of most projects (by law it cannot fund more than 50 percent). Again, this limits the ability to make a difference at the margin. Direct subsidies work best when they are applied on principles that *differ* from the other visions governing resource allocation. The NEA should be trying to fund projects that otherwise would perish or never come about in the first place. The NEA should be more like a venture capitalist.

Third, the NEA should be free to assist for-profit artistic enterprises. Much of the American cultural dynamism of the last two centuries has come in for-profit forms. Government funders, by encouraging the nonprofit organization, are making the American art world more bureaucratic.

Finally, we could relax peer review for many direct subsidies. The quality of NEA panel members is very high, but the peers are organized into panels. The very notion of a group elevates the importance of consensus. If an arts agency is to spur innovation, a good question is the following: how many individuals have the ability to veto a project decision? The greater the number of potential veto players, the less likely that innovation will occur. We therefore might consider smaller peer panels as a means of taking more chances.

8. If these changes should prove politically impossible, it would be best to "play it safe" with the NEA and other sources of direct subsidy. This would suggest a concentration of effort on preserving and showcasing the artistic heritage of mankind. Institutions such as the National Gallery of Art maintain very high levels of quality. For reasons explained in chapter 2, many of the standard inefficiencies of government are minimized when there is general agreement about product quality.

The least advantageous outcome is when an arts agency tries to be all things to all people, and is forced to spend its money to win political support. Most of all, an arts agency should have a clear sense of vision and mission. A given program should focus on either innovation or preservation.

9. The value of "accountability" is often counterproductive when applied to direct subsidies for art. To be sure, accountability is critically

important in many contexts. For instance CEOs should be accountable to shareholders. But we do not stress accountability in every sphere of human activity. For instance, tenured college professors are not (usually) accountable to university administrators for the content of their ideas. Instead we believe that an ethic of academic freedom will best promote the mission of the university. Supreme Court justices are not accountable for the content of their decisions, although Congress may respond by passing new laws, or the Constitution may be amended.

Along these lines, direct subsidies stand the greatest chance of making a positive difference when they are insulated from many pressures of accountability. We should return to the stylized facts about artistic discovery, namely that there are many failures for every success. Too much direct accountability causes the funder to be excessively afraid of failure. This limits risk taking and in the longer run limits the number of successes. Accountability works best when the quality of the average outcome is a good indicator of the tails of the distribution; this is not generally the case with the arts.

For related reasons, greater transparency of government policy is not in every way desirable. It may be better not to have too much explicit debate over arts policy, especially if that debate takes place in a centralized forum. We do not wish to put all of arts policy "on the table," so to speak. We might end up with a planned arts policy, which is probably not a better arts policy. Right now there is little danger that various American arts policies will be rationalized or coordinated, and this is probably for the better. We should be suspicious of any attempt to plan American arts policy from the top down.

10. We should consider revitalizing cultural outreach programs. These policies have been a success in the past, and they could play a future role in improving America's world image. Furthermore there is a cosmopolitan argument for such programs as a form of foreign aid. If there is any group of people who lack access to the full array of the world's cultural treasures, it is the citizens of the poorer countries or of tyrannized countries.

That all having been said, where do those recommendations come from? Why have I settled on those recommendations and not others?

## Which Arguments for Subsidies
## Remain on the Table?

The opening chapter portrayed decentralization and prestige as the two strongest factors militating in favor of subsidies of some kind or another. Let us start first with decentralization. We will see where the argument has succeeded, and how it can lead to the policy conclusions presented above.

The decentralization argument suggested that the government encourage a diversity of funding sources for art. This provides a potential rationale for several aspects of current American arts policy, such as current tax law and a strong system of higher education, as discussed in chapter 2. These policies expand the base of financial support for the arts, and decentralize funding sources, while avoiding excess politicization.

The analysis of this book does not allow us to conclude that current tax and university subsidies are good policies, all things considered. I have not examined the effects of those policies outside the arts, such as on economic growth and on education more directly. Nonetheless these indirect subsidies have been good for the arts.

Note that the decentralization argument for indirect subsidies avoids or at least deflects many of the critiques of government involvement in the arts. Drawing on earlier discussions, I will refer to the politicization critique, the libertarian critique, and the "What about the Haitians?" critique.

We have seen that indirect subsidies bring only a minimum of outside government interference. Any arts policy faces the standing danger that governments will try to control, regulate, and politicize art, but indirect subsidies have sidestepped this problem for the most part.

Tax breaks for the arts deflect the libertarian critique, although they do not eliminate it. The libertarian critique claims that individuals should not be forced to pay for arts they do not approve of. The libertarian might find it objectionable, for instance, that a conservative Christian is forced, through coercive taxation, to support an exhibit of Robert Mapplethorpe photos. Most indirect subsidies, however, do not support art in this manner.[1]

More important, the arguments of this book have not ruled out pro-posed libertarian reforms. Libertarians have (nonartistic) reasons for opposing government coercion. Some of the indirect subsidies referred to in chapter 2 rely on government coercion (university subsidies), but many others do not (tax breaks). As noted, the concept of an indirect subsidy can be interpreted quite generally. The very enforcement of law and order counts as an art subsidy in a general sense. Similarly, government policies that promote prosperity also boost the arts, and qualify as indirect subsidies under the most general definitions of that term.

To whatever extent we find libertarian arguments persuasive, we can limit the scope of indirect subsidies accordingly. Personally I am not persuaded by the view that coercion is necessarily morally wrong, nor do I think that all taxation is coercive. Therefore I evaluate indirect subsidies on a pragmatic, case-by-case basis. But if desired, the libertar-ian view could be superimposed on the policy recommendations of this book, thereby limiting indirect subsidies to the noncoercive variety. The libertarian view could not be superimposed on a regime of direct subsidies, which necessarily involve coercion in the libertarian sense. The libertarian should thus favor indirect subsidies over direct subsi-dies. The libertarian of course wishes to go further, and restrict the content of those indirect subsidies. I have left this further step as an open, and nonartistic, question.

Finally, the decentralization argument has the greatest chance of standing up to the "What about the Haitians?" critique. As we saw in chapter 1, any program of arts expenditure can be compared to a pro-gram that might save lives abroad by remedying poverty. Current arts subsidies, if redirected toward humanitarian ends, could save thou-sands of lives. Why should we prefer more opera performances to this lifesaving alternative? Subsidy proponents like to note how much the government wastes in other areas, and how small arts expenditures are in comparison, but these anecdotes do not answer the basic question.

The decentralization argument has a potential response to this query. The decentralization argument does not recommend direct sub-sidies to the arts per se. Indirect subsidies to nonprofits and to universi-ties benefit the arts only indirectly as a by-product of other, more general effects. Nonprofits and universities are arguably part of some broader effort to make the world a better and more humane place. So they might be among the best charitable investments we can make.

This response does not defuse the "What about the Haitians?" critique altogether. At the margin we still have the choice of redirecting funds away from nonprofits and toward poor Haitians. The overall comparison, however, has changed. The comparison is no longer "opera performance versus food for Haitians." The comparison is now "investing in decentralization and nonprofits as a way of improving society" versus "investing in direct charity as a means of improving society." This latter comparison places less burden on the arts and is more likely to be morally justifiable. Investing in decentralization brings a broad bundle of goods, both artistic and nonartistic in nature, many of which are humanitarian in nature.

We see also that wealthy, decentralized societies are in the best position to digest and assist immigrants. Immigration is the most effective antipoverty program. The migrants not only enjoy higher standards of living; they send billions of dollars back home in the form of remittances. The scientific discoveries of wealthy, decentralized societies also redound to the benefit of poorer regions of the world. Building up charity, and thus creative discovery, in wealthy countries therefore serves as an antipoverty program as well.

## What Aesthetic Claims Underlie the Decentralization Argument, or What Is Art?

The decentralization argument sidesteps many difficult and perhaps unresolvable questions about aesthetics. Unlike most arguments for art subsidies, the decentralization argument does not require an explicit account of why the arts are special. The resultant policy implications do not in fact treat the arts as special. Nor does the decentralization argument require a clear dividing line between artistic and nonartistic activity, an assertion that the high arts are more than a minority taste, or a declaration that the arts are especially noble or elevating. It requires only an argument for decentralization more generally, and for government support for creative energies and philanthropy. Additional support for the arts serves as one component of such a broader bundle of diverse and decentralized outputs. I take seriously and literally Walt Whitman's claim that "the United States themselves are essentially the greatest poem."[2]

Direct subsidies cannot handle these questions with equal finesse. Once we consider the possibility of subsidies for art, the question arises as to which forms of art will count. It is very difficult to demarcate artistic activities in a way that is useful for policy, or would be persuasive to either broader audiences or to philosophical specialists. This does not refute the case for direct subsidies, but it does argue for the primacy of a more indirect approach, as outlined in the previous chapters.

When the NEA was created in 1965, one conservative representative, H. R. Gross of Iowa, offered an amendment to provoke debate. The amendment, rejected out of hand, would have expanded the definition of art to include belly dancing, baseball, football, golf, tennis, squash, pinochle, and poker. This was considered a joke at the time, but the question remains as to what should count as art.[3]

Clothes, at least in their fine form, are arguably a form of art. They exhibit beauty, a refined sense of aesthetics, and they please the eye. Master designers have many of the same skills that artists have, and they face many of the same aesthetic and economic problems. The Metropolitan Museum of Art has shown Versace dresses and Cartier jewelry, while the Guggenheim has shown Armani clothes.[4]

Furthermore, attractive clothes yield external benefits for individuals other than the wearer. A well-dressed woman or man pleases many viewers, including those who are not part of the intended audience, thus producing a positive external effect. Given that clothes designs do not receive copyright or patent protection, market failure in the realm of fashion may be an especially pressing problem. If the creation of one designer is "ripped off" by another, there is no standard recourse under law. And like art, clothes shape broader social and aesthetic attitudes.

Nonetheless it is rarely argued that the government should subsidize the sale of attractive clothes. Such a policy, however, would not be difficult to implement. Clothing above a certain dollar value could be exempt from sales tax, to give one example of how the subsidy might work. The government could go further and subsidize leading design- ers on the basis of peer review, thus creating a new branch of the NEA. Clothing and design firms could be exempt from taxes, much as to- day's nonprofits are.

The question remains why "culture" should receive different policy treatment than clothing. If beauty and the aesthetic are central con- cerns, or if market-failure arguments are central to the case for subsi- dies, the case for subsidizing good clothing ought to be relatively strong.

Similarly, the government might subsidize personal looks. The gov- ernment could provide direct or indirect assistance to the producers of skin creams, plastic surgery, Rogaine, and personal deodorant. How- ever much individuals sometimes pretend to the contrary, they take pleasure in seeing other good-looking people.

Sports are, first and foremost, a form of drama. They present protag- onists, a setting, and a clash of wills. The end of the "story" brings a res- olution and a denouement. The drama in sports, of course, is real rather than staged, but presumably this should contribute to its aes- thetic merit. On top of this, many sports activities, such as figure skat- ing and basketball, are aesthetically appealing to their spectators for their beauty, grace, and spontaneity.

Governments do, of course, support sports through stadium subsi- dies at the state and local levels. But the primary argument for these subsidies is economic in nature, to stimulate community development. Rarely is it argued that government should guarantee access to profes- sional sports, but it is frequently argued that government should guar- antee access to high culture.

Arguably an academician, if he or she sat down to do so, could find qualities that distinguish sports from some narrower definition of cul- ture. We could peruse the philosophical literature on aesthetics for help. But should those differences matter for public policy? Does our reluctance to subsidize clothes, or sports, really hinge on whether these academic distinctions are persuasive?

It is commonly said that institutions such as the NEA bring the arts to democracy, but direct subsidy partisans are less keen to bring democracy to the arts. That would mean a greater role for sports and clothing in our notion of the government-supported aesthetic, and a smaller role for opera and contemporary abstract art.

When it comes to *dreaming*, it may be said that every individual is an artist. Dreams tell stories, involve metaphor and allegory, and are often quite beautiful. The best dreams may be witty or ironic. And like the other arts, dreams can mesh terror and beauty to great aesthetic effect. Dreams would seem to qualify as art in many or most regards. Of course only a single individual is allowed in the theater and taping is impossible, but why should this matter?

A variety of harmless drugs stimulate dreaming or stimulate the ability to remember one's dreams. Given a commitment to beauty and the aesthetic, to what extent is government obliged to subsidize these drugs? Dreams allow us to live in a world where, along the lines of a Marxian or Trotskyite fantasy, every individual labors daily (nightly) as an artist.

We might go further and postulate that sex is akin to art. It has drama, beauty, and enriches our lives. Warren G. Harding once opined, "A pretty girl naked is worth all the statues in the world."[5]

And what about toys? The artistic education of children is one of the chief rationales for the NEA and for government involvement in the arts more generally. The goal of policy is to turn children into supporters and consumers of high culture, as that concept is currently understood. It is a far lower priority to ensure that children, in their time as children, enjoy matters aesthetic as they understand and prefer them.

Most young children are deeply concerned with matters aesthetic. They are fascinated by colors, shapes, sounds, and textures. Most of all, they love toys. Some toys are huge successes, while most are complete failures in the marketplace. Of the six-thousand or so new toys released every year, most disappear from the market quickly and never return. The difference between success and failure lies not only in the fun of the toy but in whether the toy satisfies the aesthetic sense of enough children. The toy presents the child with an aesthetic package, so to speak, which the child either loves or rejects. When children love a toy, they are truly passionate about enjoying its aesthetic qualities.[6]

Yet it is rarely suggested that the government subsidize the purchase, production, or invention of toys. To make the matter more striking, there is arguably a market failure in the toy industry; as in fashion, competitors can copy the idea behind a new toy, if not its exact form. This externality implies that markets will produce fewer kinds of new toys than would be optimal.

For whatever reason, the aesthetic behind toys simply does not count as an argument for toy subsidy. It is considered entirely permissible, and indeed desirable, for the aesthetic dimension of toys to remain in the private sphere and outside government concern.

Jean Dubuffet perhaps went furthest in challenging the dividing line between traditional forms of high art and the aesthetic experiences of everyday life. He viewed true culture as subversive, individualistic, and standing outside social convention. He viewed "the professor" as enshrining a static sense of high culture, much as a corrupt priest would promote religion for purposes of social control. True culture, in his view, proliferates horizontally, and in many hidden channels of everyday life, rather than through a vertical structure of hierarchy and prestige.

Dubuffet noted that "culture has become identified with institutionalism." He viewed artistic vocabularies and canons as "blatantly simplifying, isolating a notion from all others to which it is connected, tending to immobilize that which is mobile, to fix that which is constantly moving, to deliver the notion stripped of the play of light that shines on it, transforming it into a simple figure, a mere extinguished echo, impoverished and denatured." The construction of artistic aura places art in the hands of academicians and prestige seekers, where Dubuffet believed it does not belong.[7]

The decentralization argument does not require such a strong skepticism about aesthetic hierarchies; nonetheless Dubuffet's position yields a further boost to the case for the primacy of indirect subsidies. Surely it is desirable when policy, however indirectly, helps deliver interesting life experiences to individual human beings. This suggests a greater concern with the aesthetic in very general terms, and less concern with the narrow definition of art. In other words, I wish to take seriously the questions of why we do not subsidize toys, dreams, sports, sex, and clothes, among other manifestations of the aesthetic, rather than just subsidizing high art. The American government should support a proliferation of creative visions in all walks of life. To extend direct subsidies to quasi-artistic areas, however, would make government into a tyrannical central planner, concerned with virtually every facet of human existence. We are again led to indirect support for a very general notion of creativity, based on the idea of decentralized funding.

## The Prestige Argument

The decentralization argument has suggested the primacy of indirect subsidies over direct subsidies. A remaining question is whether the prestige argument might overturn this conclusion, and I believe that the answer is no for several reasons.

First, many individuals, especially in the United States, enjoy living under a regime where government does *not* provide much direct support to the arts. Government involvement brings negative prestige to these individuals, perhaps because it reminds them of socialism, or forces them to identify the arts with government bureaucracy. Polls on this issue indicate mixed results. While most polls show a majority of the American public in support of arts subsidies, this majority does not typically exceed 60 percent, and sometimes pollsters do not find a majority in support. So the prestige element, in net terms, is likely to be correspondingly small.[8]

Second, and more conceptually, societies may *overinvest* in prestige and auras. This would militate against using government policy to further prestige goals.

Robert H. Frank offers one version of the overinvestment argument. In his work individuals spend too much time and energy investing in relative status. To provide a simple example, we might buy expensive art to impress our friends and play one-upsmanship, but if many others do the same, at the end no one is much happier. Frank argues that such investments are zero- or negative-sum games, akin to arms races. If we apply Frank's perspective to arts policy, it could be argued that we seek too much prestige in our state. Both the French and the Americans, for instance, might use arts policy to make their states look better in the international arena. This, too, might be a zero-sum game.[9]

Furthermore the arts expenditures that produce governmental prestige may subsidize wasteful prestige-seeking in the private sector. Subsidizing the opera, for instance, may be supporting a form of zero-sum social climbing. Elites may use the aura of high art to exclude outsiders and to reinforce social distinctions. To the extent individuals use the aura of art to cement their control of social institutions, to enforce hierarchy, or to exclude others, these activities are not purely productive. The activities, to some extent, are helping one group of individuals better their lot at the expense of others.[10]

I have written critically about Frank's argument elsewhere (see Cowen 2000, chap. 5) and do not wish to recapitulate that discussion here. My conclusion was that status competition is commonly positive-sum rather than zero- or negative-sum. The reputation of one person, or institution, is not necessarily achieved at the expense of the reputation of another. I argued we need not fear competition for prestige or status, or regard it as wasting significant resources. For this reason I do not dismiss the prestige argument on the grounds that prestige seeking is zero-sum. That being said, Frank's analysis should at least raise our skepticism about the need to *subsidize* prestige seeking through government, and through government arts policy. In other contexts we argue whether we should *tax* such behavior, not whether we should subsidize it. We already produce plenty of prestige and aura through a market economy, and we are already keen to find prestige and aesthetic value in our state. Governments need not encourage status seeking any further.

Note that this suspicion of aura and prestige does not militate against direct and indirect subsidies (decentralization) with equal force. Decentralization, by definition, will promote many different values, including aura and prestige. We should not cavil if we do not like all the values that are promoted. Recall that I am arguing for decentralization *as a bundle* that includes both artistic and nonartistic outputs. If we could pick and choose the best parts of the bundle as we saw fit, we would not need decentralization in the first place. For this reason I would hesitate to seek to fine-tune the decentralization subsidies and weed out the embedded support for aura and prestige. Fine-tuning of this kind is likely to backfire on the very rationale for decentralization in the first place, namely the difficulty of evaluating good ideas in centralized fashion. Furthermore my suspicion of aura and prestige is a weak one. Aura and prestige are not harmful, and we should not mind if a general blossoming of creativity also brings more aura and prestige. Aura and prestige simply do not require deliberate state subsidy in the artistic context.

Note an irony in the prestige argument. Arts policy would bring less prestige if it were viewed explicitly in prestige-producing terms. It is not very prestigious to seek prestige. Successful production of prestige, through arts policy, thus requires a certain unawareness of the prestige argument itself. It would require false belief about why we have direct subsidies to the arts.

## Agreeing to Disagree?

We can now revisit the initial question of why it is so hard to find agreement about arts policy. That is, why do people not recognize their own fallibility—a process I call meta-rationality—and adjust their views accordingly, moving closer to the opinions of their opponents? Why has dialogue proven so fruitless in this area?

Arts policy is not just about matters of fact. Arts policy is also about the aesthetic. It is about what kind of state we find beautiful or appealing. Advocates of direct subsidies enjoy a state that is about sweetness and light, and makes a bold statement in favor of the elevating powers of art and the importance of the artist. Many critics of direct subsidies enjoy a state that is about virtue, classical artistic values, and fiscal responsibility. For many conservatives this vision is explicitly Christian; for libertarians it is attached to the idea of individual rights.

Meta-rationality does not apply to matters of taste. I might, in a matter of fact or science, recognize that others are as smart as or smarter than I am, and defer to their judgments. But if somebody tells me I like ketchup when I do not, I will not listen, no matter how strong the credentials of the speaker. In similar fashion, arts policy is in part a matter of taste. If I prefer the Beatles and you prefer The Rolling Stones, how should we proceed? I might play you my favorite Beatles songs, cite a few critics on the virtues of the Beatles, or talk about their millions of devoted fans. But you probably know this evidence already, and my strategy is unlikely to work. We would each be left pointing to our favorite music, unable to reach agreement. Aesthetic disagreement and political disagreement have much in common.

The factor of pride makes agreement yet more difficult. In part we hold political views, and adhere to an aesthetic of the state, to feel good about ourselves and about our identifications. Participants in the arts policy dialogue—on all sides—therefore are prone to self-serving belief. This general feature of human behavior is especially pronounced in politics. We want to feel pride in our loyalties. And when our goal is to feel good about ourselves, self-deception is especially likely. People typically do not wish to put their sources of pride up for rational debate. They prefer to discard negative information and focus on the positive. Each side does not always want to hear what the other side has to say. For these reasons our arguments appear stronger to ourselves than they really are, and they will be that much harder to revise through dialogue.

Our need for aura and prestige makes us more likely to shut out critics. Those who criticize our point of view—whether about art or government—threaten to unmask its mystery. Both the left-wing "feel good about the elevating powers of art" stance and the right-wing "patriotism and virtue" stance are based on aura. Defenders of each aesthetic instinctively sense the fragility of that mystery and aura, and thus they do not wish to listen too closely to the critics. Each side erects mental and psychological defenses against the arguments offered by the other. The very debate threatens the aura that each side seeks to produce, and thus the debate does not get very far. "Feeling good about oneself" is not something that is produced very well by putting it up for regular debate.

So instead of listening, each side reinterprets the debate in a way to feel better about its own point of view. Each side vilifies the other, turning the criticism it receives into a badge of honor. Conservative Christians railed against the NEA for promoting immorality and homosexuality. Robert Hughes, in his *Time* magazine defense of arts funding, had harsh words for the Republican Congress of 1994. He described the Republican project as "cultural defoliation" and wrote, "These boys and girls aren't even cultural Neanderthals. They're Jurassic."[11]

Arguments for decentralization and indirect subsidies may, of course, be based on illusion and self-deception as well. It would be possible to construct a self-deceiving version of the decentralization argument, rooted ultimately in, of all things, prestige. If we overvalue the regime of decentralization and indirect subsidies, we will feel better about limiting direct subsidies than we ought to. We will be happier with our resulting state—representing a modern vision of a classical liberal ideal—than we ought to be. We will be working backward from a classical liberal vision of the state, and then trying to twist the analysis of arts policy to make ourselves feel good about that vision. We would be engaged in precisely that kind of enterprise that underlies some applications of the prestige argument for direct subsidies, albeit from a different political position.


## Arts and the Liberal Order: What Is Culturally Central?


The political vision of this book asks many individuals, especially art lovers and critics, to make a leap. We must resist the temptation to find too much of our aesthetic satisfaction in the state as a source of direct subsidies. Instead the role of the state is to support a legal and institutional framework—emphasizing a market economy and indirect subsidies—in which broad and diverse notions of the aesthetic can flourish. Yet demands for aura and prestige will never go away. Our aesthetic longings must therefore identify with the broader order, rather than with the state per se. The state becomes an enabler, not a doer, and thus is less directly cloaked in the aura of the aesthetic.

We can see the resulting tension. On one hand we believe that the aesthetic is of great importance and that it pervades human life, not just the arts as narrowly defined. On the other hand the proposal requires a considerable separation of the state from direct planning of the aesthetic. This separation may well redound to our long-run aesthetic, economic, and political benefit. Nonetheless it requires us to think rationally and instrumentally about the aesthetic, rather than romantically, as we are so often inclined to do.

At the end of the day, this vision will work only if it can offer some culturally central values, a set of (possibly true) myths for our times. These values should be capable of commanding wide public adherence, offer the possibility of inspiration, and mesh with American politics, economics, and religious beliefs.

The American arts themselves would not appear to offer adequate centrality. After all, we have seen that a wealthy capitalist economy tends to bring quite a diversity of artistic visions. The cultures of church and village may have been central to medieval Europe, but it is less clear what should count as fulfilling this role today.

"Popular culture" is the obvious candidate for such centrality, but I do not wish to take this route. First, popular culture is not as well defined as is commonly believed. We have television, movies, music, computer games, best sellers, fashion, and many other popular arts. Arguably celebrities could be considered a form of popular culture as well, in addition to their role in producing or carrying cultural products. Do these disparate spheres of activity offer centrality? Rap music, country music, and television situation comedies not only differ from each other greatly, but each offers more internal diversity than is usually realized. These genres offer entertainment, sadness, tragedy, visceral excitement, violent anger, and many diverse moods. Furthermore the so-called mass audience is fragmenting over time. Network television viewing is down sharply. DVDs, the Internet, and cable TV, all of which allow for greater individual choice, are displacing mass culture. File sharing and satellite radio are limiting the relevance of Top 40, and so on. As outlined in chapter 4, we can expect these decentralizing trends to continue and intensify.

Second, many commentators interpret contemporary popular culture as based on a kind of depravity. These criticisms cite excess consumerism, excess individualism, and an obsession with immediate self-gratification. Often popular culture is opposed to the idea of a liberal or classical education. I view these criticisms as wrong or overstated (Cowen 1998), but that is not the point at hand. These very perceptions make it harder to build a polity with the (perceived) values of popular culture at its center.

So if many Germans see Bach and Goethe as central to their cultural heritage, and plan their arts policy accordingly, what is the American equivalent? How can an argument for decentralization produce a coherent cultural vision to bind a liberal polity together?

I nominate three (interrelated) values as culturally central to the liberal vision of this book:

### 1. *Innovation*

As a culture we should value and reward the ability of individuals, including artists, to strike out on new paths. Openness to innovation is commonly perceived as an American value, relative to the attitudes of other countries.

### 2. *Entrepreneurship*

As a culture Americans recognize and admire the ability of ambitious individuals, including artists, to change the world for the better. Often we refer to these individuals as entrepreneurs. We seek, however imperfectly, to maximize opportunities for these individuals.

### 3. *Charity and Generosity*

Americans are the most generous private donors in the world, including to the arts. As outlined in chapter 2, they have given time, money, energy, and vision to the nonprofit sector in unprecedented magnitudes. Furthermore this attachment to charity is rooted deeply in American culture.

I am not suggesting that these are the only values that are culturally central to the United States; rather they are the values most relevant to the artistic vision of this book. Other values such as religion, patriotism, and business enterprise also underpin the American polity. But it is easiest to see how the three values listed above fit into the policy recommendations of this book. American arts policy has valued innovation, encouraged artistic entrepreneurs, and has stimulated charitable giving. Furthermore these values all find resonance with a broader American public, whether or not we are thinking about the arts. These values are firmly rooted in American history and laws. They are not mere ephemera, but rather they can provide a foundation for a self-image and for national pride.

It is not my purpose to define these values with exact clarity. Debates over the meaning of the "entrepreneurship" concept, for instance, can rapidly turn mind-numbing. Most important, some rough version of these values can serve as a central and inspiring vision for a polity. Visions of cultural centrality will never command unanimity over key terms, and in fact centrality requires a certain amount of ambiguity and creative reinterpretation from different points of the political spectrum. Nor need most individuals appreciate the abstract workings of American arts policy, or the workings of American society more generally. Rather individuals must identify emotionally with the underlying values, as listed above, and enjoy the concrete manifestations of such an order. This is not an impossible requirement.

So with these values in mind, we can revel in the creations of American society, artistic and otherwise. And if this vision succeeds, it can align the decentralization and prestige arguments to work in tandem. A market economy, and a preponderance of indirect subsidies, would now bring greatest prestige in addition to the most effective instrumental outcomes for the arts and the economy. All the arguments would come together and point in a common direction.

## Poetry and Philosophy Revisited

If we think in terms of a broader mythmaking enterprise, where should we stand on the "longstanding quarrel between philosophy and poetry," as Plato called it? The very notion of a book on the arts suggests at least a partial alliance with philosophy, rather than poetry. It is not merely lack of artistic talent that has prevented me from expressing my ideas with a painting or a musical composition; rather here poetry comes under the scrutiny of philosophy. Philosophy, in the broad sense, was used to weaken or downgrade one of the arguments for subsidizing art, namely the status and aura argument. Economics—in this context another form of philosophy—was added to the mix to weaken the arguments for investment in the aesthetic at all costs.

But under an alternative reading of this work, poetry fares better. What appear to be arguments "against" poetry are more accurately arguments against other people's philosophies about poetry. Poetry (i.e., the arts) is in fact rarely discussed directly in this book. Instead I discuss why some philosophies about poetry should shape arts policy and why others should not. The suspicion of the status and aura arguments can be seen as suspicion of false art, or suspicion of false views of art, rather than suspicion of art per se.

In a decentralized system, much of the aesthetic will be furtive and hidden to many outside observers, rather than obvious. Many of the "arts," if we can continue to use that term, will be pursued outside formal art worlds. Jean Dubuffet remarked: "True art always appears where we don't expect it, where nobody thinks of it or utters its name. Art detests being recognized and greeted by its own name. It immediately flees. Art is a character infatuated by the incognito." Ironically, today art is hidden, in part, because we find it in so many places and in so many different forms. Most manifestations of the aesthetic are not explicitly recognized as such in arts policy debate.[12]

Given that so much of the aesthetic is hidden, what appears to be the subordination of poetry to philosophy is an illusion, albeit a creativity-enhancing illusion. Rather than subordinating poetry to philosophy, at most I have subordinated the public conception of art to philosophy. Poetry remains secure in its diverse and hidden niches, and indeed is healthiest when philosophy directs the public conception of art toward a regime of markets, indirect subsidies, and decentralization. In this sense we can put philosophy at the service of art, and not at war with it. I wish to overturn the victory that Socrates pretended to award to philosophy over poetry, and to paint an alternative vision of the broader compatibility between the two enterprises.

# Notes

## 1. Warring Perspectives

1. Throughout this book I will use "U.S." and "American" interchangeably, for expositional reasons. I do not wish to deny that other "American" countries exist in this hemisphere.

2. The best-known political theorists of the Anglo-American tradition—Hobbes, Locke, Hume, and Madison, to name a few—are concerned primarily with the practical dimension of politics, rather than with the aesthetic or the imaginative. They ask how political order is possible, how property rights should be defined, and how the general welfare can be secured. A focus on politics and the aesthetic brings many of us to less familiar territory, including Vico's *New Science*, Kant's *Critique of Judgment*, the British Hegelians, John Dewey's *Experience and Art*, Eric Voegelin, and Hans-Georg Gadamer's *Truth and Method*, among other works. For two later works drawing on this tradition for an account of politics, see Arendt (1982), who was working on these issues when she died, and Beiner (1983). The best single source is Ankersmit (1996). Samuel Fleischacker (1999) reads Adam Smith as standing in this same tradition.

3. See "Would You Give Up TV for a Million Bucks?" (1992).

4. See Arnold (1993, p. 81). Varian (1992) offers one standard treatment of modern microeconomics.

5. On a right to culture, see, for instance, Arian (1989). For the quotation, see Haacke (1992, p. 146).

6. See Cwi (1982, p. 85).

7. See Musgrave and Musgrave (1989) on the theory of merit goods.

8. On this point, see Dworkin (1985, chap. 11).

9. See Richard Posner (1980) and Dworkin (1980).

10. See Schlesinger (1990, p. 5).

11. Cited in Zeigler (1994, p. 164). British author Kingsley Amis has expressed a similar sentiment; see Pick (1991, p. 89).

12. On the dollar figures, see Mangione (1972, p. 369). On the seen and the unseen, see Bastiat (1850).

13. I am assuming that the funds were invested on December 31, 1934, in the S&P 90 (the S&P 500 does not go back that far). The data are taken from www.globalfindata.com.

14. Heilbrun and Gray (1993), among other sources, provide a good survey of how various externality arguments apply to the arts.

15. On Purcell, see Dorian (1964, pp. 431–32). Grampp (1989) provides the best modern survey of externalities arguments. For an early and prescient presentation of various subsidy arguments, see Shee (1811).

16. For a collection of views on such impact studies, see *Economic Impact of the Arts: A Sourcebook* (1987).

17. The multiplier conflates the spending of money with the creation of real economic value through production. Spending causes money to pass from one set of hands to another, but that is not the same as an increase in real production. To calculate the true multiplier, we must ask what acts of net production are encouraged by a given arts investment, not how much spending it causes in gross terms. To give an example, if I build a railroad, it may produce more real economic value by raising the value of other assets; the multiplier will be positive. Conversely, I might run into the street and throw a rock at a pane of glass. The shopkeeper will spend more money to buy a new window, the window manufacturer will in turn buy more bread, the baker will buy more of some other commodity, and so on. In dollar terms there will appear to be a multiplier, but in real terms there will be no additional creation of economic value, unlike with the railroad. Often it is argued that investing in stadiums will revitalize struggling areas or cause parts of a town to boom. In reality the evidence indicates that stadium subsidies fail to stimulate economic growth at the level of cities or states. See, for instance, the survey by Siegfried and Zimbalist (2000).

18. A more complex analysis indicates a number of cases. For instance, the price of attracting an artistic cluster may be lower than the value of that cluster. In that case, however, the region with the winning bid will gain but the rest of the world may not. If price does not reflect value, the winning bidder is not necessarily bringing resources to their most highly valued uses. Cowen (2004) goes through this case, and others, in greater detail. In the empirical literature stadiums have received the most attention.

19. In philosophy the works of Derek Parfit (1984) and Thomas Hurka (1993) explore the notion that many of our moral intuitions are perfectionist

and thus implicitly antiegalitarian. In terms of data, Netzer (1992) rebuts the common presumption that the NEA involves a significant transfer of income to richer individuals, although the net effect is still antiegalitarian.

20. Unger (1996) argues for lower estimates.

21. Whether Hayek intended his own argument as a plea for laissez-faire is less clear. On a variety of issues Hayek is more "interventionist" than many of his followers, though in this case the textual evidence is ambiguous.

22. See Spence (1976) for one version of this argument; Dixit and Stiglitz (1977) present related results.

23. See Shee (1811, p. xiii, passim). Nearly all the subsequent arguments for arts subsidies can be found in Shee's remarkable work, much of which is presented in poem form.

24. On the Netherlands, see Montias (1984, p. 439), and on flower-arranging subsidies, see Shikaumi (1970, p. 27).

25. The degree of aura can change over time. Outsider and Naïve art have achieved much more aura over the last thirty years. Photography, in its early days, was seen as a substitute for portraiture and had to fight for its stature as a fine art. Moving in the other direction, coins and medal making were once considered fine arts but now command little mainstream artistic attention.

26. On the Benton episode, see McKinzie (1973, p. 3).

## 2. INDIRECT SUBSIDIES: THE GENIUS OF THE AMERICAN SYSTEM

1. Pick (1988, p. 60).

2. On international comparisons, see also Frey and Pommerehne (1989, p. 21). Frey and Pommerehne (1989, pp. 22, 68) offer the direct comparisons cited. See also Jane Alexander (2000, p. 317). On the Louvre, see "When Merchants Enter the Temple" (2001). European museums are moving closer to the American model, albeit slowly.

3. See Johnson (1997, p. 9); the data refer to 1995. On foundations, see Dowie (2001, p. 169). Some of the discussion and figures from the next few pages draw on Cowen (2005).

4. See *Giving USA* (2003, pp. 195–97). On the French comparison, see Archambault (1997, p. 208).

5. For data on itemizations, see http://ftp.fedworld.gov/pub/irs-soi/ 98db02nr.xls. On the origins of the charitable deduction, see Clotfelter (1985, pp. 31–32).

6. See Clotfelter (1985, chap. 2, and p. 274).

7. See Wyszomirski (1999, p. 186), Cobb (1996, p. 13), and *Report* (1997, p. 14) for estimates of time donations and the implicit value of time. See Clotfelter (1985, chap. 4) for a survey of some inconclusive results of how much the income tax stimulates time donations.

8. Some provisions of the tax law have hurt artists. This includes the taxation of fellowship awards and unemployment compensation (both instituted in 1986), disallowance of income averaging (which had helped artists with volatile incomes), and the 1986 restrictions on in-kind deductions for artworks given to museums. But for the most part the American tax system subsidizes the arts significantly.

9. See Frey and Pommerehne (1989, p. 43), and on England, see Clotfelter (1985, pp. 96–97). Schuster (1989, p. 33) catalogs some of the tax privileges that European governments have granted to the arts since the Second World War.

10. On American donations to the United Kingdom, see Vogel (2000). On France and Italy, see Archambault, Boumendil, and Tsyboula (1999) and Barbetta (1999).

11. The source is http://www.nasaa_arts.org/new/nasaa/nasaanews/ foundation_giving.shtml, citing an estimate by Grantmakers in the Arts, in conjunction with the Foundation Center. For the complete list of leading foundations, see Cobb (1996, p. 35). For other estimates of foundation assets, see Mehrling (1999) and Dowie (2001, p. 271).

12. See Dowie (2001, pp. 174–75).

13. On support for higher education, see Dowie (2001, p. 26).

14. See Mehrling (1999) for general information on the 5 percent requirement, and also Clotfelter (1985, chap. 7).

15. On the 1981 shift, see Mehrling (1999, p. 5). On the regulation of foundations in other countries, see *Associations and Foundations* (1998) and Edie (1987). On the pre-1969 regime, see *Treasury Department Report* (1965), Salamon and Voytek (1989, p. 6), and Troyer (2000), who also provides the figure on business-linked charities. Sweden, Germany, Spain, and Finland have partial payout requirements, see van Veen (2001, p. 712), typically consisting of a certain percentage of income rather than assets. On Belgium, see Marée and Mousny (2001); on Austria see Bachstein and Badelt (2001). On Ford, see Bulmer (1999, p. 42).

16. Mehrling (1999), for instance, recommends an increase in the payout rate. Rick Cohen (2000) estimates the spending boost that would result. On the Peterson Commission, see Odendahl and Feeney (1999). On the 1960s debates, see Dowie (2001, pp. 15–17). Note also that various expenses are covered in the 5 percent figure, so by no means is all of this grants; sometimes less than 4 percent is grants (see Dowie 2001, pp. 261–62).

17. See Mehrling (1999).

18. See Grimes (1995).

19. See Grimes (1995).

20. See Caves (2000, p. 252) and Navarro (1988).

21. On giving by negative-publicity industries, see Martorella (1990, p. 32) and Wu (2002). On public relations budgets, see Wyszomirski (1999, p. 185); on Philip Morris, see Haacke (1992, p. 141).

22. If we use the average tax rate, the potency of corporate tax incentives appears to be quite high, less so for the marginal rate. The marginal rate is the technically correct magnitude, but difficulties in measuring the true marginal rate suggest that the average rate is sometimes the better proxy. See Clotfelter (1985, chap. 5) on these issues.

23. On Artspace, and these associated subsidies, see Conlogue (2000).

24. For this information, see *Creative America* (1997, p. 4).

25. That is from the National Center for Education Statistics; see http://nces.ed.gov/pubs2005/2005356.pdf.

26. In 1974 a California representative, Thomas Rees, introduced a bill to Congress that would have made private purchases of art tax-deductible. The bill would have required the Treasury to issue formal rulings on who counts as a "professional artist" or not (see Weil 1983, pp. 195–96).

27. The governmental definition of a nonprofit institution has not led to much direct interference in artistic content decisions. Some of the more specific legal interventions arguably have been beneficial. The courts, for instance, have rendered various decisions against the Barnes Institute in Merion, Pennsylvania. The Barnes Institute is best known for its French and Modernist paintings, collected by the eccentric Albert Barnes in the early part of the twentieth century. The original terms of the Barnes bequest stipulated that the paintings would be available for public view but only on a limited basis, at certain times and to particular individuals, at the discretion of the museum. It was later ruled that this provision violated the nonprofit status of the parent institution, causing the museum to move to open public admission.

28. The NEA differs from HUD precisely because the NEA is so small. The gains from making the agency corrupt are inconsequential, relative to the potential costs. Furthermore, NEA decisions are monitored by peer reviewers, drawn from arts communities, who hold most of their reputational capital outside the government. The NEA therefore has avoided the corruption of HUD. The NEA is a best-case scenario for direct funding, whereas HUD is a worst-case scenario.

29. See Schelling (1996) on research by accident. On the influence of McElroy, see Gillies and Cailliau (2000, pp. 11–12). On the origins of the Internet, see Abbate (1999), and Gillies and Cailliau (2000) on European subsidies to research on the World Wide Web.

30. On federal R & D expenditures, see Suplee (2000).

31. See Rosenberg (1982) and Wagnleitner (1994, pp. 240–41).

32. See Goldstein (2000, pp. 59, 89, 109).

33. See Hess (1974, pp. 134–35) and Harris (1999, p. 115) on smuggled artworks.

34. See Paul Starr (2004) and p. 142 on the change in the book rate, pp. 261–62 on changes in the magazine rate. On postal subsidies, see Cummings (1991, pp. 40–41).

35. For a brief history of these taxes, see http://www.turnoffyourtv.com/international/bbc.html.

36. On radio history, see Paul Starr (2004, pp. 226–67).

37. I read McChesney (1999, p. 142) as taking this position; he also offers an estimate of $100 billion for the rights. Free allocation of the spectrum to commercial broadcasters is an arts subsidy only if we believe that the private sector is not the only potential recipient of the spectrum. Some individuals believe that the spectrum is naturally the property of the government, or they believe in some notion of the public trust. In this sense spectrum allocation to the private sector is an enormous subsidy to commercial culture, at the expense of whatever alternative the public sector would have provided. The key difference here, though, is allocating the spectrum to the private sector at all. In terms of artistic content, giving the spectrum away does not differ much from selling the spectrum.

38. On Indian policy debates, see, for instance, Fixico (1986).

39. On the historical links between American music and American churches, see Stowe (2004).

40. On architecturally notable American churches, old and new, see Howe (2003).

41. The Serrano price is taken from artnet.com; the work was sold at Christie's, May 2000.

42. See Hamilton (2000, chap. 1).

43. See Hamilton (2000, chap. 1).

44. See Franklin (1978, p. 233).

45. On prison art, see Kornfeld (1977, pp. 37, 77, passim) and Cleveland (1992).

46. On this figure, see Cleveland (1992, p. 125). The number has since fallen dramatically; by 1988 it was down to 150,000.

47. On Ramirez, see Colin Rhodes (2000, p. 113), Ippolito (1999), and the plaques at the American Visionary Art Museum in Baltimore.

48. For a general history of the American university and the arts, see the rather thin treatment by Morrison (1973). On some of the above examples, see Risenhoover and Blackburn (1976, p. 9). On Frost, see Parini (1999, pp. 206–7).

49. On Lichtenstein and Segal, see Marter (1999).

50. On O'Keeffe, see Lisle (1997, chap. 4, pp. 100–101). On Styll, see Lucie-Smith (1999, pp. 244–45).

51. Hamilton (2000, p. 31).

52. On UC Davis, see Arenson (2002).

53. See Arenson (2002).

54. See Hamilton (2000, p. 169).

55. For a comprehensive listing of these museums, see Russell and Spencer (2000).

56. On college radio, see Papish (2002).

57. On faculty growth, see Noll (1998, p. 3); on enrollment parity, see Arthur Cohen (1998, p. 302).

58. See Arthur Cohen (1998, pp. 292, 393), Trow (1993, p. 40), and Page and Simmons (2000, pp. 194–95). The 14 percent figure is from Arthur Cohen (1998, p. 394).

59. Cohen and Noll (1998, pp. 36–37).

60. See Page and Simmons (2000, pp. 194–95), and Trow (1993, pp. 43, 59–61) for some earlier numbers. On the details and history of various student aid programs, see Gladieux and Hauptman (1995).

61. Page and Simmons (2000, p. 195).

62. Trow (1993, pp. 57–58).

63. Trow (1993, pp. 58–59).

64. See the remarks of Rosovsky (1990, pp. 33–34).

65. Marsden (1994, pp. 3, 167).

66. On MIT graduates, see Arthur Cohen (1998, p. 419). For a defense of the American university, see Frank Rhodes (2001).

67. Cited in Risenhoover and Blackburn (1976, p. 21).

68. Cited in Risenhoover and Blackburn (1976, p. 24).

69. See Cotter (2000).

### 3. Direct Subsidies:
#### Are They Too Conservative?

1. On the opponents, see Kammen (2000, p. 16); on Sloan, see Penkower (1977, p. 96). On Auden, see Auden (1993). See also Kauffman (1990). On 1970 applications, see Netzer (1980, p. 59). On the 1953 poll, see Cummings (1982, p. 157). See also Hart (1973, chap. 15).

2. On these commissions, see Fairman (1927), Cosentino and Glassie (1983), Cummings (1991, pp. 33–34), Wetenhall (1988, p. 1), and Kennon (2000). On sculptural commissions during this time, see Craven (1968).

3. On the Smithsonian, see Hellman (1966), Levy (1997, pp. 20–21), Dupree (1957, chap. 4), and Meyer (1979, pp. 46–47). On Buchanan, see Netzer (1980, p. 53). On surveys of the Indian arts, see Dupree (1957, pp. 199–207). On the Tarnsey Act, see Bogart (1989, p. 75). On the National Commission, see Levy (1997, pp. 41–46) and Wetenhall (1988, p. 30). On the Roosevelt episode, see Ganz (1998, pp. 187–88).

4. For the figures and program summaries, see Cummings (1991, pp. 41–42) and Dows (1972, p. 12). In 1933 painter George Biddle sent a letter to FDR, his former roommate in prep school. Biddle cited government support for murals in Mexico and suggested that the United States government should do something comparable for the American arts (Cummings 1991, p. 41). On total expenditures, see Mangione (1972, p. 369), and on the arts projects see Zeigler (1994, p. 6). On FERA, see Netzer (1980, p. 54). On PWAP, see Contreras (1983). Bustard (1997) provides a good readable survey of the era's arts policies.

5. On the ineligibility of most artists, see Netzer (1980, pp. 54–55), and on the poverty requirements, the importance of the income, and age, see O'Connor (1971, pp. 70–71, 84, 92).

6. Naifeh and White (1998).

7. See Charles Alexander (1980, p. 211) and Mathews (1980, p. 310), among other sources.

8. See O'Connor (1971, pp. 106–7).

9. See Nunn (2001).

10. See Gonzales and Witt (1996, pp. 1, 33–35, 47–48, passim).

11. On the writers' project, see Mangione (1972, passim) and Zeigler (1994, p. 6).

12. Levy (1997, p. 68). On communists in the WPA, see Mangione (1972) and Levy (1997, p. 66).

13. Zeigler (1994, p. 6) and Charles Alexander (1980, p. 207). On Schumann and Carter, see McDonald (1969, p. 624).

14. Zeigler (1994, p. 6). On Eliot, see Lynes (1983, p. 292). On Miller, Odets, and Kazan, see Jane Alexander (2000, p. 73).

15. See Bustard (1997, pp. 12–14) on the programs in general and Daniel (1987) on the USDA program, with the quotation from Daniel, p. 41.

16. See Netzer (1980, p. 57) on the failure to institutionalize the WPA.

17. On the Swiss experience, see Overmyer (1939, p. 66).

18. Kreidler (2000, p. 167n).

19. Wyszomirski (1999, p. 135).

20. See Wagnleitner (1994, p. 72) and Pommerin (1996, p. 9). On censorship in Japan, see Dower (1999, chap. 14).

21. The numbers are taken from Wagnleitner (1994, p. 57) and drawn from U.S. budget data.

22. Snyder (1995, p. xi).

23. For a summary of the Smith-Mundt Act, and other relevant legislation, see Henderson (1969, pp. 302–7). On the genesis of the very complicated network of overlapping agencies, see Henderson (1969). On the roots in the 1930s, see Thompson and Laves (1963, pp. 36–37) and Shuster (1968).

24. Snyder (1995, p. xi).

25. Wagnleitner (1994, pp. 61, 149). On the 1969 estimate, see Henderson (1969, p. 75). Ironically many of the funds for these cultural outreach programs were taken from the "Counterpart Funds" from the Marshall Plan, and thus paid for by European taxpayers, not American taxpayers. (European governments had to put up money for each dollar received through Marshall Plan aid.) In essence, the Europeans were bribed to spend money on American cultural producers, so that they might be swayed to the American way of life. See Wagnleitner (1994, p. 57). On USIA more generally, see Elder (1968). In 1985 the USIA budget was

$796 million, many times larger than the NEA allocation. On the post-Reagan decline in these programs, see Kinzer (2001).

26. On the USIA estimate, see Coombs (1964, pp. 59–60). On audience size, see Browne (1982, p. 116). See also Wagnleitner (1994, pp. 61, 210–11) and Hixson (1997, pp. 115–17).

27. See Wagnleitner (1994, pp. 61, 210–11) and Hixson (1997, pp. 115–17). Heil (2003) is a good source on VOA. I am indebted to Bryan Caplan for the phrase "artistic famine relief." Richmond (2003) surveys cultural exchange programs, with an emphasis on their impact on the Soviet Union.

28. See von Eschen (2000 and 2004) on jazz and the State Department, and Saunders (1999, pp. 20, 291) and Hixson (1997, p. 137) on African-American issues.

29. See, for instance, Richmond (2003, p. 124) on these exchanges.

30. On these programs, see, for instance, Wyszomirski (1999, p. 126).

31. See Fine and Whiteman (2002) on Sawa's origins; on criticisms, see Kessler (2004).

32. See MacFarquhar (2004).

33. See Heil (2003, pp. 296–98).

34. On the importance of federal support for these arts, see Lowry and Hooker (1968) and von Eschen (2000, passim, p. 167). On Ailey, see Dunning (1996, pp. 145–255). On Gillespie, see Maggin (2005, chaps. 27, 28) and von Eschen (2004, p. 35).

35. On the CCF, see Saunders (1999), Coleman (1989), and Berghahn (2001).

36. On the penetration of foundations, see Saunders (1999, pp. 134–35); on books, see p. 245.

37. See Saunders (1999, pp. 257–68), Guilbaut (1983).

38. Wagnleitner (1994, pp. 137–38). On USIA, see Wetenhall (1992, p. 145).

39. Lasch (1969, p. 348).

40. See von Eschen (2000, pp. 166, 171) and Mathews (1976, p. 771, passim).

41. On Dondero, see Mathews (1976, pp. 772–73).

42. On the music festival, see Saunders (1999, p. 223).

43. DiMaggio (1984, p. 92).

44. Note that for both Mapplethorpe and Serrano the NEA had made earlier grants to each individual artist, though not for controversial works

of the kind that received the subsequent criticism. See Munson (2000, p. 71).

45. See Trescott (2000) and Farhi (2001) on the number of visitors and Wyszomirski (1999, pp. 126–27) on the number of museums. The next few pages draw on Cowen (2005).

46. On Smithsonian fund-raising, see Trescott (2000). On the federal appropriation, see Puente (2003) and also the Smithsonian Web site, www.si.edu.

47. On the expansion under Ripley, see Meyer (1979, pp. 44–47).

48. On the origins of the National Gallery, see *National Gallery of Art* (1966) and Kopper (1991). On the murky details of the tax fraud issue, see Kopper (1991, pp. 110–11). On current National Gallery funding, see Trescott (2002).

49. On programming see Jerold Starr (2000, pp. 26–27).

50. Jerold Starr (2000, pp. 25–26). On the change in CPB, see Auletta (2004).

51. Wyszomirski (1999, pp. 127–28).

52. On AiA, see Thalacker (1980) and Wyszomirski (1999, pp. 125–26). On the use of the New Deal model, see Wetenhall (1992, p. 156). The yearly budget figure is taken from an e-mail from Susan H. Harrison, who works in the AiA office.

53. See Balfe (1995, pp. 194–96) and Thalacker (1980, p. xii). On the evolution of AiA selection procedures, see Wetenhall (1988, pp. 430–47).

54. On the trust, see Allen (2000).

55. On the NEH, see Miller (1984).

56. On all these activities, see Schrader (1983) and Philp (1977).

57. See Schrader (1983, pp. 141–42).

58. On the history of the army collection, see Sullivan (1991); on works held and also on the navy collection, see Evans (1946, app. 2). The most famous war pictures of an American artist are those by John Singer Sargent (*Gassed* is the best known), although these were commissioned by the British authorities, not the American government. On Sargent's war work, see Little (1998).

59. On the USO, see Fawkes (1978, chap. 9, and p. 122) and the USO Web site, www.uso.org/about_uso.htm.

60. Wyszomirski (1999, p. 177). On Sousa, see Overmyer (1939, p. 155) and Crawford (2001, pp. 457–58). On bands, see Trescott (1995).

61. See DiMaggio (1991, pp. 217–23).

62. For the aggregate data, see *Legislative Appropriations Annual Survey* (2003, p. 3) and Cowen (2005, p. 5). On these developments, see Kinzer (2004). On the peak figure, see Timberg (2003). Schuster (2002) surveys the entire field of state arts spending.

63. Figures on expenditures are taken from the National Assembly of State Arts Agencies. On the history of state art commissions, see Purcell (1956, pp. 40–42). On New York state relief programs in the 1930s, see O'Connor (1971, pp. 30–31). See Wyszomirski (1999, p. 198n) on Utah. For a more historical study of related questions, see Hofferbert and Urice (1985).

64. On all these differences, see DiMaggio (1991).

65. See Mulcahy (1987, p. 317) and Cummings and Katz (1987, p. 365). The information on line-item appropriations is taken from mimeographed sheets from the National Assembly of State Arts Agencies, titled "SAA Legislative Line Items, Fiscal Years 1979 to Present," and also *Legislative Appropriations Annual Survey* (2001), also published by the National Assembly.

66. *United States Urban Arts Federation Fiscal Year 2002* (2002, p. 3). See also Cowen (2005, pp. 6–7).

67. On this era, see Purcell (1956, pp. 38–40).

68. This information is taken from Kreisberg (1979, pp. 7–8).

69. On New York City and the arts, see Bogart (1989, pp. 155–57).

70. See Pogrebin (2002 and 2003).

71. See Midgett (2000, p. 32) for the quotation.

72. All this information is taken from Midgette (2000).

73. On how subsidies have discouraged entrepreneurial filmmaking in Europe, see Cowen (2002, chap. 4).

74. *Within* western Europe, we may have too great a similarity of European policies, since many of those countries produce roughly the same kinds of culture. Global culture might be more interesting if the European governments could introduce more variation in their artistic environments, although no single country necessarily would benefit to introduce such variation unilaterally. European governments look first and foremost after their own citizens, rather than trying to benefit Europe as a whole.

75. Dorian (1964) provides a useful history of the European experience.

76. On Philip's patronage of Velázquez, see Cowen (1998, chap. 3).

77. On Lott, see Frohnmayer (1993, pp. 52–53).

78. See Zeigler (1994, p. 121) on the U.S. polls. Even in western Europe the support for funding is often far from unanimous. The Swiss city of Basel once held a popular referendum on whether the municipal museum should purchase some Picasso paintings. Basel is an extremely art-conscious city, by world standards, but the purchase was approved by a relatively thin margin of 53.9 percent. On Switzerland, see Frey and Pommerehne (1993, pp. 169–72).

79. On NEA structure, see, among other sources, Wyszomirski (1999).

80. This paragraph is indebted to the insightful first chapter of Munson (2000); see p. 48 on the figures. The treatment of Brenson (2001) is useful as well.

81. See Pogrebin (2001) on the increase to 40 percent.

82. On these figures, see *Report* (1997, p. 25).

83. On the Vietnam War Memorial, see Levitt (1991, p. 22), and on Chihuly, see Jane Alexander (2000, p. 173). Brenson (2001, pp. 85–86) lists a number of visual artists that the NEA has funded, many of whom have gone on to significant success.

84. On the change in vote, see Zeigler (1994, p. 138).

85. One NEA estimate was that one NEA dollar brings in eleven private dollars; see Kreidler (2000, p. 168). A private consulting firm hired by the NEA, Cultural Resources, Inc., estimated that one NEA dollar brings six private dollars; see Mooney (1980, p. 245). Note that no one forces the private sector to follow NEA giving. If the multiplier effect indeed holds, the private sector likely would seek out alternative means of reputational certification in the absence of the NEA. Prior to the NEA, for instance, receiving a grant from the Ford or Rockefeller foundations carried a great deal of clout with other donors, and often still does. The system has a conservative bias with or without government. The "centralization of taste" effect, to whatever extent it is a problem, is arguably as much a market failure as a failure of government arts policy.

## 4. COPYRIGHT AND THE FUTURE OF DECENTRALIZED INCENTIVES

1. In late 1998 Congress passed the Digital Millennium Copyright Act, which prohibits the unauthorized decryption of posted works. While this act regulates Internet-based copying in great detail, most of its provisions are already technologically obsolete. In some regards the act opens

the door for Internet copying, by limiting the liability of online service providers for copying done by their account holders.

2. See Strong (1999, p. 149). On Rodman, see Besenjak (1997, pp. 52–53).

3. A dissident branch of libertarianism, called "Galambosianism," after its founder Galambos, once advocated precisely such a system. Tom Palmer (1990 and 1997), a contemporary libertarian, suggests that no (zero) copyright protection is the natural starting point. Suppliers, however, could offer covenants to those who purchase their products. It is an open question to what extent third parties (what if the material is "lost"?) would be bound by those covenants as well.

4. On symbolic goods, see Cassirer (1975), Todorov (1982), Cowen (2000), Eric Posner (1998), and Richard Posner (2001).

5. On Proust, see http://books.guardian.co.uk/Print/0,3858,3950488, 00.html.

6. The page numbers are taken from the Amazon.com listing; of course there are many differing editions. One current Web version is at http://www.ccel.org/a/aquinas/summa/FP.html.

7. See "Learning to e-read" (2000).

8. See Mann (2000, p. 50), working from data supplied by Simon Frith. The obvious problem with this or any number is deciding who counts as a musical artist.

9. See Seabrook (2003).

10. See McPherson (1999, pp. 66–67). This does not include any royalties that must be paid to the producer, but of course Internet music does not alter this cost.

11. For more detailed information on the costs borne by record companies, see Schwartz (1997) and McPherson (1999).

12. On Fisher, see Mann (2000, p. 54).

13. On the retail estimate, see "Siren Songs" (2000, pp. 16–22).

14. Mann (2000) discusses the scenario of funding through advertisement; see Mann (2000, p. 50) for the comparison with Northwestern Mutual. On Coca-Cola, see http://biz/yahoo.com/p/k/ko.html.

15. On this switch, see Caves (2000, p. 241–42).

16. In the context of literature, William Warburton, an eighteenth-century theologian, argued that the decline of copyright would spur creativity and quality. He argued that money was a corrupting lure, and that fame incentives would provide for a superior product, as they did for

the ancients. Warburton noted approvingly Thucydides's comment that he wrote to be famous, not to be fed. On Warburton, see Cowen (1998, chap. 2). Unlike my view, Warburton hoped that copyright protection would disappear.

17. On this episode, see Crawford (2001, pp. 720–21).

18. On past museum purchases of copies, see Sassoon (2001, p. 41).

19. See Snider (2004).

20. Cowen (2002, chap. 4) offers more information and data on this history.

21. See, for instance, Walker (2000). On the revisions to the number of years of copyright protection, see also Wyszomirski (1999, pp. 129–30).

22. On Dylan, see Walker (2000).

23. On various aspects of compulsory licensing, see Samuels (2000).

24. We can also see a possible public-goods problem when the music companies set their fees for their online services. Each might tend to set fees too high. A high fee encourages more rogue services, but each single company bears only part of the cost of each rogue. Compulsory licensing, by opening up the market to competition and enforcing lower fees across the board, will require each company to give up some profits in order to make the market harder for the rogues.

25. On the Supreme Court, see Patterson and Lindberg (1991, pp. 61–62). See Rose (1993, chap. 2) and Patterson and Lindberg (1991, p. 26, passim).

## 5. Toward a Beautiful and Liberal Future

1. Tax exemptions for nonprofits do not take money from conservative Christians and send it to "obscene" exhibits. Rather, the tax breaks imply that nonprofits do not pay taxes in the first place, or that donors to nonprofits pay lower taxes. These lower taxes, whether the money is spent for morally approved ends or not, presumably meet with libertarian approval. According to the libertarian argument, purveyors of obscene material should be taxed at the lowest rate possible. In response, it might be argued that the conservative Christian is taxed indirectly to pay for the Mapplethorpe exhibit. If a Mapplethorpe-exhibiting museum pays no taxes, perhaps taxes on others will end up higher. This factual claim may or may not be true (total expenditures might be cut, rather than other taxes being raised). But even if the claim is true, the resulting libertarian injustice lies

in the tax policy, not the arts policy. It may be unjust that the tax break for nonprofits is not extended to the conservative Christian, but the tax break for nonprofits is not itself unjust by libertarian standards. Of course a moral distinction between direct subsidy and tax exemption may be implausible, and thus may be an argument against the libertarian perspective more generally. But within the libertarian perspective, which I am taking as given for the moment, the distinction between a subsidy and a tax exemption is a morally important one.

2. See Whitman (1959, p. 5).

3. On Gross, see Kammen (1997, p. 77).

4. Schaeffer (2000) and Shiner (2001) argue that the notion of "fine arts" is an arbitrary historical category, rather than a distinction based in real differences across genres.

5. See Merrill (1986, p. 344).

6. On toy failures, see Caves (2000, p. 211).

7. See Dubuffet (1988). The quotations are from pp. 71 and 46.

8. See Zeigler (1994, p. 121) on the U.S. polls. Even in western Europe the support for funding is often far from unanimous. The Swiss city of Basel once held a popular referendum on whether the municipal museum should purchase some Picasso paintings. Basel is an extremely art-conscious city, by world standards, but the purchase was approved by a relatively thin margin of 53.9 percent. On Switzerland, see Frey and Pommerehne (1993, pp. 169–72).

9. See Frank 1987.

10. Pierre Bourdieu's *Distinction* emphasizes the use of culture to enforce and define hierarchies. Sociologist Paul J. DiMaggio has written about how the "Boston Brahmins" set up nonprofits and institutions of high culture at the turn of the twentieth century. They sought to maintain some degree of influence over Boston civic life as their direct political control slipped away. On art, aura, and critics more generally, see the writings of Danto, such as Danto (1997).

11. See Hughes (1995, p. 62).

12. For the Dubuffet quotation, see Maizels (1996, p. 36).

# References

Abbate, Janet. 1999. *Inventing the Internet*. Cambridge, Massachusetts: MIT Press.

Alexander, Charles C. 1980. *Here the Country Lies: Nationalism and the Arts in Twentieth Century America*. Bloomington: Indiana University Press.

Alexander, Jane. 2000. *Command Performance: An Actress in the Theater of Politics*. New York: Public Affairs.

Allen, Kent. 2000. "Trust Finds a Less Taxing Way of Life." *The Washington Post*, May 16, p. A19.

Ankersmit, F. R. 1996. *Aesthetic Politics: Political Philosophy beyond Fact and Value*. Stanford, California: Stanford University Press.

Archambault, Edith. 1997. *The Nonprofit Sector in France*. Manchester, England: Manchester University Press.

Archambault, Edith, Judith Boumendil, and Sylvie Tsyboula. 1999. "Foundations in France." In *Private Funds, Public Purpose: Philanthropic Foundations in International Perspective*, edited by Helmut K. Anheier and Stefan Toepler. New York: Plenum, pp. 185–98.

Arendt, Hannah. 1982. *Lectures on Kant's Political Philosophy*, edited with an interpretative essay by Ronald Beiner. Chicago: University of Chicago Press.

Arenson, Karen W. 2002. "Arts Groups and Artists Find Angels: Universities." *The New York Times*, October 30, pp. B1, B8.

Arian, Edward. 1989. *The Unfulfilled Promise: Public Subsidy of the Arts in America*. Philadelphia: Temple University Press.

Arnold, Matthew. 1993 [1869]. *Culture and Anarchy and Other Writings*. Cambridge: Cambridge University Press.

*Associations and Foundations*. 1998. Strasbourg: Council of European Publishing.

Auden, W. H. 1993. *The Prolific and the Devourer*. Hopewell, New Jersey: Ecco Press.

Auletta, Ken. 2004. "Big Bird Flies Right.: How Republicans Learned to Love PBS." *The New Yorker*, June 7, pp. 42–48.

Bachstein, Werner, and Christoph Badelt. 2001. "Austria." In *Foundations in Europe*, edited Myra Bennett and Rosie Clay. London: The Directory of Social Change, pp. 84–93.

Balfe, Judith Huggins. 1995. "The Process of Commissioning Public Sculpture: 'Due' or 'Duel.'" In *America's Commitment to Culture: Government and the Arts*, edited by Kevin V. Mulcahy and Margaret Jane Wyszomirski. Boulder, Colorado: Westview Press, pp. 189–204.

Barbetta, Gian Paolo. 1999. "Foundations in Italy." In *Private Funds, Public Purpose: Philanthropic Foundations in International Perspective*, edited by Helmut K. Anheier and Stefan Toepler. New York: Plenum, pp. 199–218.

Bastiat, Frédéric. 1850. *Essays on Political Economy*. London: A. W. Bennett.

Beiner, Ronald. 1983. *Political Judgment*. Chicago: University of Chicago Press.

Benjamin, Walter. 1986. "The Work of Art in an Age of Mechanical Reproduction." In *Illuminations*. New York: Schocken Books.

Berghahn, Volker R. 2001. *America and the Intellectual Cold Wars in Europe: Shepard Stone between Philanthropy, Academy, and Diplomacy*. Princeton, New Jersey: Princeton University Press.

Besenjak, Cherul. 1997. *Copyright Plain and Simple*. Franklin Lakes, New Jersey: Career Press.

Bogart, Michele H. 1989. *Public Sculpture and the Civic Ideal in New York City, 1890–1930*. Chicago: University of Chicago Press.

Boyle, James. 1996. *Shamans, Software, and Spleens: Law and the Construction of the Information Society*. Cambridge, Massachusetts: Harvard University Press.

Brenson, Michael. 2001. *Visionaries and Outcasts: The NEA, Congress, and the Place of the Visual Artist in America*. New York: New Press.

Browne, Donald R. 1982. *International Radio Broadcasting: The Limits of the Limitless Medium*. New York: Praeger Publishers.

Bulmer, Martin. 1999. "The History of Foundations in the United Kingdom and the United States: Philanthropic Foundations in Industrial Society." In *Private Funds, Public Purpose: Philanthropic Foundations in International Perspective*, edited by Helmut K. Anheier and Stefan Toepler. New York: Plenum, pp. 27–54.

Bustard, Bruce I. 1997. *A New Deal for the Arts*. Seattle: University of Washington Press.

Cassirer, Ernst. 1975. *The Philosophy of Symbolic Forms*, two volumes. New Haven, Connecticut: Yale University Press.

Caves, Richard E. 2000. *Creative Industries: Contracts between Art and Commerce*. Cambridge, Massachusetts: Harvard University Press.

Cleveland, William. 1992. *Art in Other Places: Artists at Work in America's Community and Social Institutions*. Westport, Connecticut: Praeger.

Clotfelter, Charles T. 1985. *Federal Tax Policy and Charitable Giving*. Chicago: University of Chicago Press.

Cobb, Nina Kressner. 1996. *Looking Ahead: Private Sector Giving to the Arts and the Humanities*. Washington, D.C.: President's Committee on the Arts and the Humanities.

Cohen, Arthur M. 1998. *The Shaping of American Higher Education*. San Francisco: Jossey-Bass Publishers.

Cohen, Linda R., and Roger G. Noll. 1991. "An Assessment of R&D Commercialization Programs." In *The Technology Pork Barrel*, edited by Linda R. Cohen and Roger G. Noll. Washington, D.C.: Brookings Institution Press, pp. 365–392.

Cohen, Linda R., and Roger G. Noll. 1998. "Universities, Constituencies, and the Role of the States." In *Challenges to Research Universities*, edited by Roger G. Noll. Washington, D.C.: Brookings Institution Press, pp. 31–62.

Cohen, Rick. 2000. "Foundation Payout: Considerations and Actions for Nonprofit Executive Directors." *Nonprofit Quarterly* 7, December, pp. 31–34, 36.

Coleman, Peter. 1989. *The Liberal Conspiracy: The Congress for Cultural Freedom and the Struggle for the Mind of Postwar Europe*. New York: Free Press.

Conlogue, Ray. 2000. "From the St. Lawrence Centre to Steel City." *Toronto Globe and Mail*, June 21, p. R5.

Contreras, Belisario R. 1983. *Tradition and Innovation in New Deal Art*. Lewisburg: Bucknell, Pennsylvania: University Press.

Cooke, Brett, and Frederick Turner, editors. 1993. *Biopoetics: Evolutionary Explorations in the Arts*. Lexington, Kentucky: ICUS.

Coombs, Philip H. 1964. *The Fourth Dimension of Foreign Policy: Educational and Cultural Affairs*. New York: Harper & Row.

Cordes, Joseph J., and Robert S. Goldfarb. 1996. "The Value of Public Art as Public Culture." In *The Value of Culture*, edited by Arjo Klamer. Amsterdam: Amsterdam University Press, pp. 77–95.

Cosentino, Andrew J., and Henry H. Glassie. 1983. *The Capital Image: Painters in Washington, 1800–1915*. Washington, D.C.: Smithsonian Institution Press.

Cotter, Holland. 2000. "Jacob Lawrence Is Dead at 82; Vivid Painter Who Chronicled Odyssey of Black Americans." *The New York Times*, June 10, p. A13, Washington edition.

Cowen, Tyler. 1998. *In Praise of Commercial Culture*. Cambridge, Massachusetts: Harvard University Press.

Cowen, Tyler. 2000. *What Price Fame?* Cambridge, Massachusetts: Harvard University Press.

Cowen, Tyler. 2002. *Creative Destruction: How Globalization Is Shaping the World's Cultures*. Princeton, New Jersey: Princeton University Press.

Cowen, Tyler. 2003. "Entrepreneurship, Austrian Economics, and the Quarrel between Philosophy and Poetry." *The Review of Austrian Economics* 16, 1, pp. 5–25.

Cowen, Tyler. 2004. "When Should Regions Bid for Artistic Resources?" Unpublished manuscript, George Mason University.

Cowen, Tyler. 2005. *How the United States Funds the Arts*. National Endowment for the Arts Monograph. Washington, D.C.: National Endowment for the Arts.

Craven, Wayne. 1968. *Sculpture in America*. New York: Thomas Y. Crowell Company.

Crawford, Richard. 2001. *America's Musical Life: A History*. New York: W. W. Norton & Company.

*Creative America: A Report to the President by the President's Committee on the Arts and the Humanities*. 1997. Washington, D.C.: President's Committee on the Arts and Humanities.

Cummings, Milton C., Jr. 1982. "To Change a Nation's Cultural Policy: The Kennedy Administration and the Arts in the United States, 1961–1963. In *Public Policy and the Arts*, edited by Kevin V. Mulcahy and C. Richard Swaim. Boulder, Colorado: Westview Press, pp. 141–68.

Cummings, Milton C., Jr. 1991. "Government and the Arts: An Overview." In *Public Money and the Muse: Essays on Government Funding for the Arts*, edited by Stephen Benedict. New York: W. W. Norton & Company, pp. 31–79.

Cummings, Milton C., Jr., and Richard S. Katz. 1987. "Government and the Arts in the Modern World: Trends and Prospects." In *The Patron*

*State: Government and the Arts in Europe, North America, and Japan.* Oxford: Oxford University Press, pp. 350–68.

Cummings, Milton C., Jr., and J. Mark Davidson Schuster. 1989. *Who's to Pay for the Arts? The International Search for Models of Arts Support.* New York: ACA Books.

Cwi, David. 1982. "Merit Good or Market Failure: Justifying and Analyzing Public Support for the Arts." In *Public Policy and the Arts,* edited by Kevin V. Mulcahy and C. Richard Swaim. Boulder, Colorado: Westview Press, pp. 59–89.

Daniel, Pete. 1987. "Command Performances: Photography from the United States Department of Agriculture." In *Official Images: New Deal Photography,* edited by Pete Daniel, Merry A. Foresta, Maren Stange, and Sally Stein. Washington, D.C.: Smithsonian Institution Press, pp. 36–42.

Danto, Arthur C. 1997. *After the End of Art: Contemporary Art and the End of History.* Princeton, New Jersey: Princeton University Press.

Dewey, John. 1958 [1934]. *Art as Experience.* New York: Capricorn Books.

DiMaggio, Paul J. 1984. "The Nonprofit Instrument and Influence of the Marketplace." In *The Arts and Public Policy in the United States,* edited by by W. McNeil Lowry. Englewood Cliffs, New Jersey: Prentice Hall, pp. 57–99.

Dimaggio, Paul J. 1991. "Decentralization of Arts Funding from the Federal Government to the States." In *Public Money and the Muse: Essays on Government Funding for the Arts,* edited by Stephen Benedict. New York: W. W. Norton & Company, pp. 216–52.

Dissanayake, Ellen. 2000. *Art and Intimacy: How the Arts Began.* Seattle: University of Washington Press.

Dixit, Avinash K., and Joseph E. Stiglitz. 1977. "Monopolistic Competition and Optimum Product Diversity." *American Economic Review* 67, 3, June, pp. 297–308.

Dorian, Frederick. 1964. *Commitment to Culture.* Pittsburgh: University of Pittsburgh Press.

Dower, John W. 1999. *Embracing Defeat: Japan in the Wake of World War II.* New York: W. W. Norton & Company.

Dowie, Mark. 2001. *American Foundations: An Investigative History.* Cambridge, Massachusetts: MIT Press.

Dows, Olin. 1972. "The New Deal's Treasury Art Program: A Memoir." In *The New Deal Art Projects: An Anthology of Memoirs,* edited by Francis V. O'Connor. Washington, D.C.: Smithsonian Institution Press.

Dubuffet, Jean. 1988. *Asphyxiating Culture and Other Writings.* New York: Four Walls Eight Windows.

Dunning, Jennifer. 1996. *Alvin Ailey: A Life in Dance.* Reading, Massachusetts: Addison-Wesley.

Dupree, A. Hunter. 1957. *Science in the Federal Government: A History of Policies and Activities to 1940.* Cambridge, Massachusetts: Harvard University Press.

Dworkin, Ronald M. 1980. "Is Wealth a Value?" *Journal of Legal Studies* 9, pp. 191–226.

Dworkin, Ronald M. 1985. "Can a Liberal State Support Art?" In *A Matter of Principle.* Cambridge, Massachusetts: Harvard University Press.

*Economic Impact of the Arts: A Sourcebook.* 1987. Denver: National Conference of State Legislatures.

Edie, John A. 1987. "Congress and Foundations: Historical Summary. "In *America's Wealthy and the Future of Foundations*, edited by Teresa Odendahl. New Haven, Connecticut: The Foundation Center, pp. 43–64.

Elder, Robert E. 1968. *The Information Machine: The United States Information Agency and American Foreign Policy.* Syracuse, New York: Syracuse University Press.

Evans, Grace Orvis. 1946. "Sources of Historic and Contemporary American War Art." Master's thesis, University of Minnesota.

Fairman, Charles E. 1927. *Art and Artists of the Capitol of the United States of America.* Washington, D.C.: United States Government Printing Office.

Farhi, Paul. 2001. "Smithsonian Sets Visitor, Donation Records." *The Washington Post*, January 23, pp. C1, C4.

Fawkes, Richard. 1978. *Fighting for a Laugh: Entertaining British and American Armed Forces, 1939–1946.* London: MacDonald and Jane's.

Feld, Alan L., Michael O'Hare, and J. Mark Davidson Schuster. 1983. *Patrons Despite Themselves: Taxpayers and Arts Policy.* New York: New York University Press.

Feist, Andrew, and Robert Hutchison, editors. 1990. *Cultural Trends 1990: Funding the Arts in Seven Western Countries.* London: Policy Studies Institute.

Ferry, Luc. 1993. *Homo Aestheticus: The Invention of Taste in the Democratic Age.* Chicago: University of Chicago Press.

Fine, Janet, and Bobbie Whiteman. 2002. "U.S. Plans Arab TV Net." *Variety*, October 14–20, p. 25.

Fixico, Donald L. 1986. *Termination and Relocation: Federal Indian Policy, 1945–1960*. Albuquerque: University of New Mexico Press.

Fleischacker, Samuel. 1999. *A Third Concept of Liberty: Judgment and Freedom in Kant and Adam Smith*. Princeton, New Jersey: Princeton University Press.

Frank, Robert H. 1987. *Choosing the Right Pond: Human Behavior and the Quest for Status*. Oxford: Oxford University Press.

Franklin, H. Bruce. 1978. *The Victim as Criminal and Artist: Literature from the American Prison*. New York: Oxford University Press.

Frey, Bruno S., and Felix Oberholzer-Gee. 1998. "Public Choice, Cost-Benefit Analysis, and the Evaluation of Cultural Heritage." In *Does the Past Have a Future? The Political Economy of Heritage*, edited by Alan Peacock. London: The Institute for Economic Affairs. pp. 27–53.

Frey, Bruno S., and Werner W. Pommerehne. 1989. *Muses and Markets: Explorations in the Economics of the Arts*. Cambridge, Massachusetts: Basil Blackwell.

Frohnmayer, John. 1993. *Leaving Town Alive: Confessions of an Arts Warrior*. Boston: Houghton Mifflin.

Fryd, Vivian Green. 1992. *Art and Empire: The Politics of Ethnicity in the U.S. Capitol, 1815–1860*. New Haven: Yale University Press.

Ganz, David L. 1998. *The World of Coins and Coin Collecting*. Chicago: Bonus Books.

Geist, Bill. 2001, "A Military Disaster Waiting to Happen." *The New York Times*, November 11, Weekend, p. 14.

Gillies, James, and Robert Cailliau. 2000. *How the Web Was Born: The Story of the World Wide Web*. Oxford: Oxford University Press.

*Giving U.S.A.* 2003. Bloomington, Indiana: American Association of Fundraising Counsel.

Gladieux, Lawrence E., and Arthur M. Hauptman. 1995. *The College Aid Quandary: Access, Quality, and the Federal Role*. Washington, D.C.: Brookings Institution Press.

Goldstein, Malcolm. 2000. *Landscape with Figures: A History of Art Dealing in the United States*. Oxford: Oxford University Press.

Gonzales, Edward, and David L. Witt. 1996. *Spirit Ascendant: The Art and Life of Patrocino Barela*. Santa Fe: Red Crane Books.

Grampp, William D. 1989. *Pricing the Priceless: Art, Artists, and Economics*. New York: Basic Books.

Grimes, William. 1995. "Business Said to Put More in Arts." *The New York Times*, October 12, pp. C15, C23.

Guilbaut, Serge. 1983. *How New York Stole the Idea of Modern Art: Abstract Expressionism, Freedom, and the Cold War*. Chicago: University of Chicago Press.

Haacke, Hans. 1992. "Beware of the Hijackers!" In *Culture and Democracy: Social and Ethical Issues in Public Support for the Arts and Humanities*, edited by Andrew Buchwalter. Boulder, Colorado: Westview Press, pp. 139–54.

Hamilton, John Maxwell. 2000. *Casanova Was a Book Lover, and Other Naked Truths and Provocative Curiosities about the Writing, Selling, and Reading of Books*. Baton Rouge: Louisiana State University Press.

Hampshire, Stuart. 2000. *Justice Is Conflict*. Princeton, New Jersey: Princeton University Press.

Harris, Leo J. 1999. "From the Collector's Perspective: The Legality of Importing Pre-Columbian Art and Artifacts." In *The Ethics of Collecting Cultural Property: Whose Culture? Whose Property?* edited by Phyllis Mauch Messenger. Albuquerque: University of New Mexico Press, pp. 155–75.

Hart, Philip. 1973. *Orpheus in the New World: The Symphony Orchestra as an American Cultural Institution*. New York: W. W. Norton & Company.

Heil, Alan L., Jr. 2003. *Voice of America: A History*. New York: Columbia University Press.

Heilbrun, James, and Charles M. Gray. 1993. *The Economics of Art and Culture: An American Perspective*. Cambridge: Cambridge University Press.

Hellman, Geoffrey T. 1966. *The Smithsonian: Octopus on the Mall*. Philadelphia: J. B. Lippincott Company.

Henderson, John W. 1969. *The United States Information Agency*. New York: Frederick A. Praeger Publishers.

Herbst, Jurgen. 1982. *From Crisis to Crisis: American College Government, 1636–1819*. Cambridge, Massachusetts: Harvard University Press.

Hess, John L. 1974. *The Grand Acquisitors*. Boston: Houghton Mifflin.

Hixson, Walter L. 1997. *Parting the Curtain: Propoganda, Culture and the Cold War, 1945–1961*. New York: St. Martin's Press.

Hofferbert, Richard I., and John K. Urice. 1985. "Small-Scale Policy: The Federal Stimulus versus Competing Explanations for State Funding of the Arts." *American Journal of Political Science* 29, 2, May, pp. 308–29.

Holcombe, Randall. 2000. *Writing Off Ideas: Taxation, Foundations, and Philanthropy in America*. New Brunswick, New Jersey: Transaction Publishers.

Howard, Donald S. 1973. *The WPA and Federal Relief Policy*. New York: Da Capo Press.

Howe, Jeffery. 2003. *Houses of Worship: An Identification Guide to the History and Styles of American Religious Architecture*. San Diego: Thunder Bay Press.

Hughes, Robert. 1995. "Pulling the Fuse on Culture." *Time*, August 7, pp. 61–68.

Hurka, Thomas. 1993. *Perfectionism*. Oxford: Oxford University Press.

Ippolito, Jon. 1999. "Collection in Focus: Recognition and Rescue, the Tale of the Martinez Ramirez Drawings at the Guggenheim Drawings at the Guggenheim Museum." *Guggenheim*, Fall, pp. 6–9.

Jaffee, Adam B. 1989. "The Real Effects of Academic Research." *American Economic Review* 79, 5, December, pp. 957–70.

Johnson, Arthur T. 1997. "Symphony Orchestras and Local Governments." Working paper, Maryland Institute for Policy Analysis and Research, University of Maryland Baltimore County.

Kammen, Michael. 1997. *In the Past Lane: Historical Perspectives on American Culture*. Oxford: Oxford University Press.

Kammen, Michael. 2000. "Culture and the State in America." In *The Politics of Culture: Policy Perspectives for Individuals, Institutions, and Communities*, edited by Gig Bradford, Michael Gary, and Glenn Wallach. New York: New Press, pp. 114–40.

Kaufmann, Bill. 1990. "Subsidies to the Arts: Cultivating Mediocrity." Cato Policy Analysis, Washington, D.C., August 8.

Kennon, Donald R., editor. 2000. *The United States Capitol: Designing and Decorating a National Icon*. Athens: University of Ohio Press.

Kessler, Glenn. 2004. "The Role of Radio Sawa in Mideast Questioned." *The Washington Post*, October 13, p. A12.

Kinzer, Stephen. 2001. "The Untold Story: Why They Don't Know Us." *The New York Times*, November 11, Weekend, p. 5.

Kinzer, Stephen. 2004. "Many State Arts Councils Make Their Case and Survive Budget Cuts." *The New York Times*, January 8, pp. B1, B8.

Kluge, P. F. 1993. *Alma Mater: A College Homecoming*. Reading, Massachusetts: Addison-Wesley Publishing Center.

Kopper, Philip. 1991. *America's National Gallery of Art: A Gift to the Nation*. New York: Harry N. Abrams.

Kornfeld, Phyllis. 1997. *Cellblock Visions: Prison Art in America*. Princeton, New Jersey: Princeton University Press.

Kreidler, John. 2000. "Leverage Lost: Evolution in the Nonprofit Arts Ecosystem." In *The Politics of Culture*, edited by Gigi Bradford. New York: New Press, pp. 147–68.

Kreisberg, Luisa, editor. 1979. *Local Government and the Arts*. New York: American Council for the Arts.

Larson, Gary O. 1983. *The Reluctant Patron: The United States Government and the Arts, 1943–1965*. Philadelphia: University of Pennsylvania Press.

Lasch, Christopher. 1969. "The Cultural Cold War: A Short History of the Congress for Cultural Freedom." In *Towards a New Past: Dissenting Essays in American History*, edited by Barton J. Bernstein. New York: Vintage Books, pp. 322–59.

"Learning to e-read." 2000. *The Economist*, October 7, p. 22.

*Legislative Appropriations Annual Survey, Fiscal Year 2003*. 2003. Washington, D.C.: National Assembly of State Arts Agencies.

Lessig, Lawrence. 2004. *Free Culture: How Big Media Uses Technology and the Law to Lock Down Culture and Control Creativity*. New York: Penguin Press.

Levitt, Arthur, Jr. 1991. "Introduction." In *Public Money and the Muse: Essays on Government Funding for the Arts*, edited by Stephen Benedict. New York: W. W. Norton & Company, pp. 19–30.

Levy, Alan Howard. 1997. *Government and the Arts: Debates over Federal Support of the Arts in America from George Washington to Jesse Helms*. Lanham, Maryland: University Press of America.

Lisle, Laurie. 1997. *Portrait of an Artist: A Biography of Georgia O'Keefe*. New York: Washington Square Press.

Little, Carl. 1998. *The Watercolors of John Singer Sargent*. Berkeley: University of California Press.

Lowell, Julia F. 2004. *State Arts Agencies 1965–2003: Whose Interests to Serve?* Santa Monica, California: Rand Corporation.

Lowry, W. McNeil, and Gertrude S. Hooker. 1968. "The Role of the Arts and the Humanities." In *Cultural Affairs and Foreign Relations*, edited by Paul J. Braisted. Washington, D.C.: Columbia Books, pp. 45–87.

Lucie-Smith, Edward. 1999. *Lives of the Great 20th Century Artists*. London: Thames and Hudson.

Lynes, Russell. 1983. *The Tastemakers*. Westport, Connecticut: Greenwood Press.

MacFarquhar, Neil. 2004. "Washington's Arabic TV Effort Gets Mixed Reviews." *The New York Times*, February 20, p. A3.

Maggin, Donald L. 2005. *Dizzy: The Life and Times of John Birks Gillespie*. New York: Harper Entertainment.

Maizels, John. 1996. *Raw Creation: Outsider Art and Beyond*. London: Phaidon Press.

Mangione, Jerre. 1972. *The Dream and the Deal: The Federal Writer's Project, 1935–1943*. Boston: Little, Brown and Company.

Mann, Charles C.2000. "The Heavenly Jukebox . . . Internet Piracy Isn't the Problem—the Music Industry Is the Problem." *The Atlantic Monthly*, September, pp. 39–59.

Marée, Michel, and Sophie Mousny. 2001. "Belgium." In *Foundations in Europe*, edited by Myra Bennett and Rosie Clay. London: The Directory of Social Change, pp. 94–102.

Marquis, Alice Goldfarb. 1995. *Art Lessons: Learning from the Rise and Fall of Public Arts Funding*. New York: Basic Books.

Marsden, George M. 1994. *The Soul of the American University: From Protestant Establishment to Established Nonbelief*. Oxford: Oxford University Press.

Marter, Joan. 1999. *Off Limits: Rutgers University and the Avant-Garde, 1957–1963*. New Brunswick, New Jersey: Rutgers University Press.

Martorella, Rosanne. 1990. *Corporate Art*. New Brunswick, New Jersey: Rutgers University Press.

Mathews, Jane de Hart. 1976. "Art and Politics in Cold War America." *The American Historical Review* 81, 4, October, pp. 762–87.

Mathews, Jane deHart. 1980. *The Federal Theatre, 1935–1939: Plays, Relief, and Politics*. New York: Octagon Books.

Max, D. T. 2000. "The Electronic Book." *The American Scholar* 69, 3, Summer, pp. 17–28.

McCarthy, Kevin, Arthur Brooks, Julia Lowell, and Laura Zakaras. 2001. *The Performing Arts in a New Era*. Santa Monica, California: Rand Corporation; also available at http://www.rand.org/publications/MR/MR1367/.

McChesney, Robert W. 1999. *Rich Media, Poor Democracy: Communication Politics in Dubious Times*. Urbana: University of Illinois Press.

McDonald, William F. 1969. *Federal Relief Administration and the Arts*. Columbus: Ohio State University Press.

McKinzie, Richard D. 1973. *The New Deal for Artists*. Princeton, New Jersey: Princeton University Press.

McPherson, Brian. 1999. *Get It in Writing: The Musician's Guide to the Music Business*. Milwaukee: Hal Leonard.

Mehrling, Perry. 1999. "Spending Policies for Foundations: The Case for Increased Grants Payout." Economics Department, Barnard College.

Merrill, Charles. 1986. *The Checkbook: The Politics and Ethics of Foundation Philanthropy*. Boston: Oelgeschlager, Gunn & Hain.

Meyer, Karl E. 1979. *The Art Museum: Power, Money, Ethics*. New York: William Morrow and Company.

Midgette, Anne. 2000. "For Singers, a New American Way." *The New York Times*, July 2, Arts and Leisure, pp. 25–32, Washington edition.

Miller, 1984. Stephen. *Excellence and Equity: The National Endowment for the Humanities*. Lexington: University Press of Kentucky.

Mohn, Tanya. 2001. "Office Artwork Brings Out the Critic in Employees." *The New York Times*, January 31, p. C10, Washington edition.

Molotsky, Irvin. 2000. "Donations May Be Sought to Send U.S. Arts Abroad." *The New York Times*, November 29, p. B3.

Montesquieu. 1989 [1748]. *The Spirit of the Laws*. Cambridge: Cambridge University Press.

Montias, J. Michael. 1984. "Public Support for the Performing Arts in Western Europe and the United Sates: History and Analysis." In *Comparative Development Perspectives*, edited by Gustav Ranis, Robert L. West, Mark W. Leisserson, and Cynthia Taft Morris. Boulder, Colorado: Westview Press, pp. 409–44.

Mooney, Michael Macdonald. 1980. *The Ministry of Culture: Connections among Art, Money and Politics*. New York: Wyndham Books.

Morrison, Jack. 1973. *The Rise of the Arts on the American Campus*. New York: McGraw-Hill.

Mulcahy, Kevin V. 1987. "Government and the Arts in the United States." In *The Patron State: Government and the Arts in Europe, North America, and Japan*. Oxford: Oxford University Press, pp. 311–32.

Munson, Lynne. 2000. *Exhibitionism: Art in an Era of Intolerance*. Chicago: Ivan R Dee.

Musgrave, Richard A., and Peggy B. Musgrave. 1989. *Public Finance in Theory and Practice*. New York: McGraw Hill.

Naifeh, Steven, and Gregory White Smith. 1998. *Jackson Pollock: An American Saga*. New York: Woodword/White.

*The National Gallery of Art: A Twenty-Five Year Report*. 1966. Washington, D.C.: National Gallery of Art.

Navarro, Peter. 1988. "Why Do Corporations Give to Charity?" *Journal of Business* 61, 1, January, pp. 65–93.

Netzer, Dick. 1980. *The Subsidized Muse: Public Support for the Arts in the United States*. Cambridge: Cambridge University Press.

Netzer, Dick. 1992. "Arts and Culture." In *Who Benefits from the Nonprofit Sector?* edited by Charles T. Clotfelter. Chicago: University of Chicago Press, pp. 174–206.

Nietzsche, Friedrich. 1956 [1870–71]. *The Birth of Tragedy*. Garden City, New York: Doubleday Anchor Books.

Noll, Roger G. 1998. "The American Research University: An Introduction." In *Challenges to Research Universities*, edited by Roger G. Noll. Washington, D.C.: Brookings Institution Press, pp. 1–30.

Nordhaus, William D. 2004. "Schumpeterian Profits in the American Economy: Theory and Measurement." NBER Working Paper #10433, April.

Nunn, Tey Marianna. 2001. *Hispana and Hispano Artists of the New Deal Era*. Albuquerque: University of New Mexico Press.

O'Connor, Francis V. 1971. *Federal Support for the Visual Arts: The New Deal and Now*. Greenwich, Connecticut: New York Graphic Society.

Odendahl, Teresa, and Diane Feeney. 1999. "Who's Afraid of Increasing Payout?" *Foundation News and Commentary* 40, 3, May/June, pp. 22, 24.

Orwell, George. 1968. *In Front of Your Nose, 1945–1950*, volume IV of *The Collected Essays, Journalism and Letters of George Orwell*. New York: Harcourt, Brace & World.

Overmyer, Grace. 1939. *Government and the Arts*. New York: W. W. Norton & Company.

Page, Benjamin I., and James R. Simmons. 2000. *What Government Can Do: Dealing with Poverty and Inequality*. Chicago: University of Chicago Press.

Palmer, Thomas G. 1990. "Are Patents and Copyrights Morally Justified? The Philosophy of Property Rights and Ideal Objects." *Harvard Journal of Law and Public Policy* 13, 3, Summer.

Palmer, Thomas G. 1997. "Intellectual Property: A Non-Posnerian Law and Economics Approach." In *Intellectual Property: Moral, Legal, and International Dilemmas*, edited by Adam Moore. New York: Rowman and Littlefield.

Papish, Michael. 2002. "College Radio, Struggling to Be Heard." *The Washington Post*, November 10, p. B2.

Parfit. Derek. 1984. *Reasons and Persons*. Oxford: Clarendon Press.

Parini, Jay. 1999. *Robert Frost: A Life*. New York: Henry Holt and Company.

Patterson, L. Ray, and Stanley W. Lindberg. 1991. *The Nature of Copyright: A Law of User's Rights*. Athens: University of Georgia Press.

Peacock, Alan. 1976. "Welfare Economics and Public Subsidies to the Arts." In *The Economics of the Arts*, edited by Mark Blaug. Boulder, Colorado: Westview Press.

Penkower, Monty Noam. 1977. *The Federal Writer's Project: A Study in Government Patronage of the Arts*. Urbana: University of Illinois Press.

Philp, Kenneth. 1977. *John Collier's Crusade for Indian Reform, 1920–1954*. Tucson: University of Arizona Press.

Pick, John. 1988. *The Arts in a State: A Study of Government Arts Policies from Ancient Greece to the Present*. Bristol, England: Bristol Classical Press.

Pick, John. 1991. *Vile Jelly: The Birth, Life, and Lingering Death of the Arts Council of Great Britain*. Cross Hill Cottage, England: Brynmill Press.

Pietan, Norman. 1949. "Federal Government and the Arts." Ph.D. dissertation, Columbia University.

Pogrebin, Robin. 2001. "A New Chief Steps In at a Changed National Endowment for the Arts." *The New York Times*, December 22, pp. A17, 29.

Pogrebin, Robin. 2002. "Institutions Brace for Cuts by the City." *The New York Times*, January 16, pp. B1, B3.

Pogrebin, Robin. 2003. "City Eases the Pain in Budget for Arts." *The New York Times*, July 2, pp. B1, B12.

Pommerin, Reiner. 1996. *Culture in the Federal Republic of Germany, 1945–1995*. Washington, D.C.: Berg.

Posner, Eric A. 1998. "Symbols, Signals, and Social Norms in Politics and the Law." *Journal of Legal Studies*, 27, 2, part 2, pp. 765–98.

Posner, Richard A. 1980. "The Value of Wealth: A Comment on Dworkin and Kronman." *Journal of Legal Studies*, 9, pp. 243–52.

Posner, Richard A. 2001. *Public Intellectuals: A Study of Decline*. Cambridge, Massachusetts: Harvard University Press.

"Public Libraries in the United States: Fiscal Year 2002." 2002. National Center for Education Statistics, http://nces.ed.gov/pubs2005/2005356.pdf.

Puente, Maria. 2003. "Smithsonian Spruces Up." *USA Today*, October 20, p. D1.

Purcell, Ralph. 1956. *Government and Art: A Study of the American Experience*. Washington, D.C.: Public Affairs Press.

Renz, Loren, and Steven Lawrence. *Arts Funding: An Update of Foundation Trends*. New York: The Foundation Center.

*Report on a Creative and Generous America: The Healthy State of the Arts in America and the Continued Failure of the National Endowment for the Arts*. 1997. Prepared for use by the Subcommittee on Oversight and Investigations of the Committee on Education and the Workforce. U.S. House of Representatives, Washington, D.C., September 23.

Rhodes, Colin. 2000. *Outside Art: Spontaneous Alternatives*. London: Thames and Hudson.

Rhodes, Frank H. T. 2001. *The Creation of the Future: The Role of the American University*. Ithaca, New York: Cornell University Press.

Richmond, Yale. 2003. *Cultural Exchange and the Cold War*. University Park: Pennsylvania State University Press.

Rifkin, Jeremy. 2000. *The Age of Access: The New Culture of Hypercapitalism, Where All of Life Is a Paid-for Experience*. New York: Jeremy P. Tarcher/Putnam.

Risenhoover, Morris, and Robert T. Blackburn. 1976. *Artists as Professors: Conversations with Musicians, Painters, and Sculptors*. Urbana: University of Illinois Press.

Rose, Mark. 1993. *Authors and Owners: The Invention of Copyright*. Cambridge, Massachusetts: Harvard University Press.

Rosenberg, Emily S. 1982. *Spreading the American Dream: American Economic and Cultural Expansion, 1890–1945*. New York: Hill and Wang.

Rosovsky, Henry. 1990. *The University: An Owner's Manual*. New York: W. W. Norton & Company.

Russell, John J., and Thomas S. Spencer. 2000. *Art on Campus: The College Art Association's Official Guide to American College and University Art Museums and Exhibition Galleries*. Monkton, Maryland: Friar's Lantern.

Salamon, Lester M., and Kenneth P. Voytek. 1989. *Managing Foundation Assets: An Analysis of Foundation Investment and Payout Procedures and Performance*. New York: The Foundation Center.

Samuels, Edward. 2000. *The Illustrated Story of Copyright*. New York: Thomas Dunne Books.

Sassoon, Donald. 2001. *Becoming Mona Lisa: The Making of a Global Icon*. New York: Harcourt.

Sassower, Raphael, and Louis Cicotello. 2000. *The Golden Avant-Garde: Idolatry, Commercialism, and Art.* Charlottesville: University Press of Virginia.

Saunders, Frances Stonor. 1999. *The Cultural Cold War: The CIA and the World of Arts and Letters.* New York: New Press.

Schaeffer, Jean-Marie. 2000. *Art of the Modern Age: Philosophy of Art from Kant to Heidegger.* Princeton, New Jersey: Princeton University Press.

Schelling, Thomas C. 1996. "Research by Accident." *Technological Forecasting and Social Change* 53, pp. 15–20.

Schlesinger, Arthur, Jr. 1990. "America, the Arts, and the Future: The First Nancy Hanks Lecture on the Arts and Public Policy." In *The Future of the Arts: Public Policy and Arts Research*, edited by David B. Pankrats and Valerie B. Morris. New York: Praeger, pp. 3–13.

Schrader, Robert. 1983. *The Indian Arts and Crafts Board: An Aspect of New Deal Indian Policy.* Albuquerque: Univeristy of New Mexico Press.

Schuster, J. Mark Davidson. 1985. *Supporting the Arts: An International Comparative Study.* Cambridge, Massachusetts: MIT Press.

Schuster, J. Mark Davidson. 1989. "The Search for International Models: Results from Recent Comparative Research in Arts Policy." In *Who's to Pay for the Arts? The International Search for Models of Arts Support*, edited by Milton C. Cummings, Jr., and J. Mark Davidson Schuster. New York: ACA Books, pp. 15–42.

Schuster, J. Mark. 1996. "Questions to Ask of a Cultural Policy: Who Should Pay? Who Should Decide?" *Culture and Policy* 7, no. 1.

Schuster, J. Mark. 2002. "Sub-national Cultural Policy—Where the Action Is? Mapping State Cultural Policy in the United States." Working paper, The Cultural Policy Center, University of Chicago.

Schwartz, Daylle Deanna. 1997. *The Real Deal: How to Get Signed to a Record Label from A to Z.* New York: Billboard Books.

Seabrook, John. 2003. "Is It Still Possible to Create a Pop Star?" *The New Yorker*, July 7, pp. 42–55.

Shee, Martin Archer. 1811. *Rhymes on Art.* Philadelphia: John F. Watson; original London, 1809.

Shikaumi, Nobuya. 1970. *Cultural Policy in Japan.* Paris: UNESCO.

Shiner, Larry. 2001. *The Invention of Art: A Cultural History.* Chicago: University of Chicago Press.

Shuster, George N. 1968. "The Nature and Development of United States Cultural Relations." In *Cultural Affairs and Foreign Relations*, edited by Paul J. Braisted. Washington, D.C.: Columbia Books, pp. 1–44.

Siegfried, John, and Andrew Zimbalist. 2000. "The Economics of Sports Facilities and Their Communities." *Journal of Economic Perspectives* 14, 3, Summer, pp. 95–114.

"Siren Songs." 2000. *The Economist*, October 7, pp.16–22.

Smith, James Allen. 2000. "Leverage Lost: Evolution in the Nonprofit Arts Ecosystem." In *The Politics of Culture*, edited by Gigi Bradford, Michael Gary, and Glenn Wallach. New York: New Press, pp. 147–69.

Smith, James Allen. 2000. "Preface." In *The Politics of Culture*, edited by Gigi Bradford, Michael Gary, and Glenn Wallach. New York: New Press, pp. ix–xi.

Snider, Mike. 2004. "DVD's Success Steals the Show." *USA Today*, January 8, pp. A1–2.

Snyder, Alvin A. 1995. *Warriors of Disinformation: American Propaganda, Soviet Lies, and the Winning of the Cold War, an Insider's Account.* New York: Arcade Publishing.

Spence, A. Michael. 1976. "Product Differentiation and Welfare." *American Economic Review* 66, 2, May, pp. 407–14.

Starr, Jerold M. 2000. *Air Wars: The Fight to Reclaim Public Broadcasting.* Boston: Beacon Press.

Starr, Paul. 2004. *The Creation of the Media: Political Origins of Modern Communications.* New York: Basic Books.

Stowe, David W. 2004. *How Sweet the Sound: Music in the Spiritual Lives of Americans.* Cambridge, Massachusetts: Harvard University Press.

Straight, Michael. 1979. *Twigs for an Eagle's Nest: Government and the Arts, 1965–1978.* New York: Devon Press.

Strong, William S. 1999. *The Copyright Book: A Practical Guide*, fifth edition. Cambridge, Massachusetts: MIT Press.

Sullivan, General Gordon R. 1991. *Portrait of an Army.* Washington, D.C.: United States Army Center of Military History.

Suplee, Curt. 2000. "Report Shows How, Where U.S. Spends R&D Funds." *The Washington Post*, June 16, p. A27.

Thalacker, Donald. 1980. *The Place of Art in the World of Architecture.* New York: Chelsea House Publishers.

Thompson, Charles A., and Walter H. C. Laves. 1963. *Cultural Relations and U.S. Foreign Policy.* Bloomington: University of Indiana Press.

Throsby, David. 1994. "The Production and Consumption of the Arts: A View of Cultural Economics." *Journal of Economic Literature* 32, 1, March, pp. 1–29.

Timberg, Craig. 2003. "D.C. Grant to Theater Starts Flood of Funding." *The Washington Post,* December 3, pp. A1, A18.

Todorov, Tzvetan. 1982. *Theories of the Symbol.* Oxford: Blackwell.

*Treasury Department Report on Private Foundations.* 1965. Washington, D.C.: Committee on Ways and Means, U.S. House of Representatives.

Trescott, Jacqueline. 1995. "NEA Hears the Beat of The Bands." *The Washington Post,* March 20, p. D7.

Trescott, Jacqueline. 2000. "Smithsonian Sets Fundraising, Attendance Records." *The Washington Post,* September 12, p. C14.

Trescott, Jacqueline. 2002. "Smithsonian Avoids Cuts, Gets $9 Million Boost." *The Washington Post,* February 3, pp. C1, C5.

Trow, Martin. 1993. "Federalism in American Higher Education." In *Higher Learning in America, 1980–2000,* edited by Arthur Levine. Baltimore: The Johns Hopkins University Press, pp. 39–65.

Troyer, Thomas A. 2000. "The 1969 Private Foundation Law: Historical Perspective on Its Origins and Underpinnings." *The Exempt Organization Tax Review* 27, 1, January, pp. 52–65.

Unger, Peter. 1996. *Living High and Letting Die: Our Illusion of Innocence.* New York: Oxford University Press.

*United States Urban Arts Federation Fiscal Year 2002.* 2002. Washington, D.C.: Americans for the Arts.

Van Veen, Wino J. M. 2001. "Supervision of Foundations in Europe: Post-incorporation Restrictions and Requirements." In *Foundations in Europe,* edited by Myra Bennett and Rosie Clay. London: The Directory of Social Change, pp. 694–743.

Varian, Hal. 1992. *Microeconomic Analysis,* third edition. New York: W. W. Norton & Company.

Vogel, Carol. 2000. "Arts Patrons with a Trans-Atlantic Reach." *The New York Times,* September 28, pp. B1, B9.

Von Eschen, Penny M. 2000. "'Satchmo Blows Up the World': Jazz, Race, and Empire during the Cold War." In *"Here, There, and Everywhere": The Foreign Politics of American Popular Culture,* edited by Reinhold Wagnleitner and Elaine Tyler May. Hanover, New Hampshire: University Press of New England, pp. 163–78.

Von Eschen, Penny M. 2004. *Satchmo Blows Up the World: Jazz Ambassadors Play the Cold War.* Cambridge, Massachusetts: Harvard University Press.

Wagnleitner, Reinhold. 1994. *Coca-Colonization and the Cold War: The Cultural Mission of the United States in Austria after the Second World War*. Chapel Hill: University of North Carolina Press.

Walker, Jesse. 2000. "Copy Catfight: How Intellectual Property Laws Stifle Popular Culture." *Reason*, March, reproduced on http://www.reason.com/0003/fe.jw.copy.html.

Webster, Sally. 1992. "Writing History/Painting History: Early Chronicles of the United States and Pictures for the Capitol Rotunda." In *Critical Issues in Public Art: Content, Context, and Controversy*, edited by Harriet F. Senie and Sally Webster. Washington, D.C.: Smithsonian Books, pp. 33–43.

Weil, Stephen E. 1983. *Beauty and the Beasts: On Museums, Art, the Law, and the Market*. Washington, D.C.: Smithsonian Institution Press.

Weil, Stephen E. 1991. "Tax Policy and Private Giving." In *Public Money and the Muse: Essays on Government Funding for the Arts*, edited by Stephen Benedict. New York: W. W. Norton & Company, pp. 153–81.

West, Edwin G. 1985. *Subsidizing the Performing Arts*. Toronto: Ontario Economic Council.

Wetenhall, John. 1988. *The Ascendancy of Modern Public Sculpture in America*. Ann Arbor, Michigan: University Microfilms.

Wetenhall, John. 1992. "Camelot's Legacy to Public Art: Aesthetic Ideology in the New Frontier." In *Critical Issues in Public Art: Content, Context, and Controversy*, edited by Harriet F. Senie and Sally Webster. Washington, D.C.: Smithsonian Books, pp. 142–57.

"When Merchants Enter the Temple." 2001. *The Economist*, April 21, pp. 64–66.

Whitman, Walt. 1959. *Leaves of Grass: The First (1855) Edition*. New York: Viking Press.

Wilson, Robin. 2000. "They May Not Wear Armani to Class, but Some Professors Are Filthy Rich." *Chronicle of Higher Education*, March 3, pp. A16–18.

"Would You Give Up TV for a Million Bucks?" 1992. *TV Guide*, October 10, pp. 10–15

Wu, Chin-Tao. 2002. *Privatising Culture: Corporate Art Intervention since the 1980s*. London: Verso.

Wyszomirski, Margaret Jane. 1999. "Background on Cultural Policies and Programs in the U.S." In *Comparing Cultural Policy: A Study of Japan*

*and the United States,* edited by Joyce Zeamand and Archie Kleingart-
ner. London: Altamira Press.

Zeigler, Joseph Wesley. 1994. *Arts in Crisis: The National Endowment for
the Arts versus America.* Chicago: a cappella books.

# Index